ANTHOLOGY

The
POETRY ChURCh
Anthology
1999

The
POETRY
church
Anthology
1999

Edited by
John Waddington-Feather

ARTHUR JAMES
BERKHAMSTED

First published in Great Britain in 1998 by

ARTHUR JAMES LTD
40 Lower Kings Road
Berkhamsted
Hertfordshire HP4 4AA

24/3/99

Compilation © John Waddington-Feather 1998
Poems © Individual authors

John Waddington-Feather asserts the moral right
to be identified as the editor of this work.

ISBN 0 85305 429 0

Typeset in Adobe Garamond by
Strathmore Publishing Services, London N7

Printed and bound in Great Britain by
The Guernsey Press Company Ltd, Guernsey, C.I.

Contents

vii

Preface

The Poetry Church goes from strength to strength; not only in the increased membership, but also in the quality and the amount of Christian poetry we receive. And equally important, in the amount of fellowship and help we give each other. With each submission, with each letter, we are making new friendships. And that is the essence of our fellowship in Christ. It goes beyond mere acquaintance.

I am very conscious as I edit or type out members' poems that I am sharing their own spiritual experience, whether it be expressed in a simple ballad or some deeply metaphysical poem or long narrative monologue. When I have finished reading or editing, I am aware of a feeling akin to worship. Perhaps that is one indication of a poem containing real Christian content. I hope the same experience is shared by our readers.

From the feedback we receive, I know that is the case with some. Time and again, readers have written to say how poems in each number of our magazine have moved them in different ways. Sometimes after a bereavement, when a poem has brought comfort. Sometimes in illness when a poem has helped healing. Occasionally in despair, when a poem or prayer has brought hope.

Earlier this year I received a telephone call from a dear friend who lived some distance away, too far to visit easily. He was terminally ill with motor neurone disease. He phoned me early in January to say he had not sent a Christmas card because he could no longer write. I felt moved to send him last year's anthology which has prayers for the terminally ill at the back. Shortly after receiving it he rang again to say how much support he was receiving from the anthology; not only from the prayers but from the poetry, too. He died in April, but I feel that in spirit he is with us still, like some of our poets who were dying when they sent us their verse.

And Sandy is but one of several who have been helped by our poetry ministry. In another instance the widow of one of our poets, whose collection we published, wrote to say how much satisfaction her husband got from seeing his verse in print before he died. More than that, she had something left to remember him by, something of him very alive.

From the start, I have felt that has been an essential part of our ministry. As a Christian church, a unique church because we are all poets who come from different denominations, we have to use our gifts to worship God first and then to help our neighbours, those who read and contribute to our magazine. We have also to evangelise, take out God's Word to others, make it meaningful to our generation. We can do that through our poetry as much as any preacher from his pulpit. Indeed, our magazine and anthology are our pulpit. We 'preach' from them and are listened to by those who often do not go near a church.

Poetry, like music, crosses all borders. It thrives on innovation and cross-fertilisation of forms and structures. It is truly international like our church. As we approach the millennium, I would like to feel our fellowship in Christ through verse and music will spread across the world. At present it is centred mainly in the States and Britain, but it is spreading and members are joining from mainland Europe and further afield week by week.

The publishing of our anthology by Arthur James Ltd will help in this growth. They have greater resources than ourselves and more expertise in the technicalities of publishing. Their distribution and editorial facilities are extensive. So is their religious booklist, which I can strongly recommend.

May God continue to bless us and all who read our magazine and its anthology in the year ahead.

REVD JOHN WADDINGTON-FEATHER

Shrewsbury, August 1998

Anchorite

I have wanted to spend
my life in two rooms.
But perhaps, in time,
going from the room of my heart
to the room of His,
perhaps, bit by bit,
the wall will crumble,
leaving no door
whose position I can choose.
Perhaps I can spend
my life in one room.

Sr Andrew-John

Blindness

They would *not* believe,
not by seeing. 'This is
the gardener,' Mary thought.
'A stranger joined us on the road,'
two of them said. Belief came
at first not by sight
but through other senses:
the spoken word, 'Mary!'
the smell of cooking fish,
a finger placed in the wounds,
the taste of broken bread.

Sr Andrew-John

Ash Wednesday

On Tuesday I put on my sackcloth robe,
reminder of my true unworthiness,
and sit down in the ashes, where I probe
my inmost self with ruthless thoroughness.
Before I throw the ashes on my head
I carefully arrange my sleeves and skirt
to best display my penitence and dread
of judgement, which I know is my desert.

On Wednesday my Lord smiles at all my woe.
'Do you not know,' says He, 'what I have done
to save you all this pain? You worry so!
Stand up! I'll brush you off. Your sins are gone.'
And so His loving touch clears all away
except this ashen cross to mark the day.

Sr Andrew-John

Communion of Saints

The men and women of my Kalendar
will share with me bits of their very bone
to keep me in their love. I know they are
not constantly alert to me alone,
yet do I ask their prayers, and always find
great comfort in their power to intercede
for me. And I might wish to get the kind
of answers that are miracles indeed!

I know I paint them as they never were;
not folks at all, but statues. Oh, how few
they were who always let their will concur
with God, Whose miracles became theirs, too.
A saint may be – or may become for me –
a mirror of the God I cannot see.

Sr Andrew-John

On John Donne

How can John Donne, long dead, give me today
the words I need to pray? And I can't see
with my own eyes the 'great unnumbered Three?'
Surely my love must tell me what to say,
though 'my devout fits come and go' the way
his did. And can I not aspire to be,
though earthbound, by my eloquence set free
'to see more in the clouds' by what I pray?

So in those moments when I feel Christ's hand
and am left breathless by His touch, I start
to look for words of thanks – pious, but grand
and 'seeking secrets' to set me apart.
Then would I soar! But I can only stand
and pray, 'O, be Thou nailed unto my heart!'

Sr Andrew-John

Greyhound

This graceful creature, long-limbed as a deer,
who loves me with his eyes, can't understand
that this five-digit thing is called a hand
that finds that special place behind his ear;
nor can he know that I can see and fear
the dangers in his world; or how I've planned
to make sure he has food. He'll only stand
and nuzzle at the god he knows is here.

So must I love what I can never name,
and only with my faulty vision see.
The world – proof of the Creator's art –
must for the moment be enough. The same
unquestioning, adoring stance must be
my own till I can step beyond my heart.

Sr Andrew-John

Monday's Prayer

She came to church for Eucharist each day,
and always sat beside her friend Arlene.
Enjoying Sunday's incense, now unseen,
she knelt on her arthritic knees to say
the old familiar prayers, the same today
as year on year of yesterdays had been.
Later, she slid on polished oak to lean
and whisper softly, 'Arlene, did I pray?'

Something's unclear. The lines of time and space
no longer can be counted on to make
the actions suited to the spoken word.
So did she pray? Indeed, age can't erase
the habits of a life of prayer, or take
away the words unspoken, but still heard.

God's Light

God shine a light,
every depth within my heart.
Promise me, my dearest Lord,
that You and I won't part.

God shine a light,
and stay close by within.
Lead me forward on my way,
and shield me from all sin.

God shine a light,
a candle in my life.
Be my Teacher, lead me forth,
save me from evil strife.

Benjamin Barton

Gardener

Considering faith,
my own issue,
I look up and wonder at the gardener of the sky.
Is he watching,
ploughing, mowing
over me?

Benjamin Barton

Listen Silently

Silently I am speaking.
Listen and widen your ears.
Silently you are around me.
Listen for God here.

Listen for God in silence.
Silently have no fear.
Listen for God around you.
Silently, for night is near.

Benjamin Barton

Innocent Joy

All at once from nowhere
he alights in the garden;
complete and singular,
a tiny lord of creation.

So bright, so confident, so frail,
you catch your breath for him
as for a little child,
lest he should come to harm.

As curious children will,
he comes closer to see;
and like a boy sudden and shrill
whistles from the bare tree.

Into our hearts he creeps
companionable and small,
and lifts our spirits up
when the dark days fall.

So bright, so confident, so frail,
a spark of life, a Christmas toy,
he comes like nature's evangel
and brings us innocent joy.

Laurie Bates

The First Easter

Sadly that first Easter would dawn
for those who nearest followed Him,
afraid He was not more than man
and left alone now He had gone.
Fear not.
Did He not say he would return.

Outside, people would talk and laugh
in the sunshine, and walk about,
but there were those who with their grief
in the upper room were shut.
Fear not.
No doors, no locks can keep Him out.

The true Christ risen from the dead,
Mary tell them what you did see;
He came amidst them where they hid,
their terrible joy on Easter Day.
Fear not.
Death itself cannot keep Him away.

Laurie Bates

Woman of Canaan

No hype, no pre-publicity,
everyday people, down-to-earth;
the presence of Divinity,
power to act where there is faith.

He saw at once what He would do:
first compassion in her trouble,
and then through this for all to know,
His Church the world, not Israel.

And the Woman of Canaan, who,
like a stout cockney streetwise wife,
matched with instinct divine IQ
and played Him for all she was worth.

And but for protocol like HM,
so grateful for what He had done,
I think she might have hugged Him
right there in front of everyone.

Laurie Bates

Forgiveness

Forgiveness is me
  looking at you
    and saying, *'I'm sorry.*
    No matter the hurt you inflicted,
    the bitter memories,
    the scars still pulling,
    weeping wounds,
    the nightmare dreams,
    I can forgive
    and love,
    and ask that from your heart
    you will forgive me, too.'

And then together
  we may face the world
  and smile,
  forgiving
  and forgiven,
  whole again.

Patricia Batstone

God's Armoury

Put on the belt of truth
around your empty waist;
gird fast your time of youth
and keep your speaking chaste.

God's breastplate round your chest
will guard against misgiving;
protection of the best,
to help you with right living.

Your feet shod with Good News,
the Gospel of release;
no chance must you refuse
to offer others peace.

Before you hold faith's shield
to ward off evil blows;
with that you'll never yield
whatever Satan throws.

And wear God's precious helm,
the helmet of salvation;
then nought can overwhelm,
no evil or temptation.

Hold fast the Spirit's sword,
to fight the goodly fight;
preach far and wide God's Word,
and battle for the right.

Throughout your mortal life
protect yourself with prayer;
in trouble and in strife,
remember Christ is there.

11

Revival

Lord, revive me your child,
bring to life my heart and mind;
curb my inclinations wild,
leave my stubborn will behind.

Set again my soul on fire
with your burning Spirit's flame;
that it might my life inspire,
glorify your holy Name.

Others, too, I then will lead
to the Spirit's gentle Dove;
helping unbelievers heed
all you brought us of God's love.

Donna Baxter

Gift Token

The message at the Gate Beautiful
of the Temple
seemed crazy
to the cripple, till the wings
of the Spirit caught him up
and he soared with the ease
of perfect health; leaping
and walking hand in hand
with Peter. The message
slips through our doors
often unopened:
'Silver and gold have I none,
but such as I have give I thee.'

Gillian Bence-Jones

Be God's Instrument

If you can make someone happy
with a kind word and a smile,
then your day is so much richer,
and your time much more worthwhile.

If you can help a friend with
no thought of personal gain,
and pray for those in sickness
and help in easing their pain.

If you call someone who's lonely
and help brighten up their day,
bringing some happiness to those
you meet along life's way.

If you overlook the hurtful words
which occasionally come your way,
forget, forgive and bless them,
they know not what they say.

Then you are being an instrument,
doing things that God would approve,
giving out your greatest portions
of God's benevolent Love!

Lucille Jean Bielak

Together for Ever

When you've always been a close couple
and the Lord then takes one away,
you're left all alone in heartache,
as you valiantly face each day.

But time goes by and you ponder,
your heart is filled with despair;
what's happened to the friends we knew?
Is it possible they don't care?

Perhaps you are an encumbrance,
you don't fit in any more
with the couples that visit together,
it can never be as before.

They turn to their other interests,
they have families of their own;
but to me, it would be a comfort
just to converse over the phone.

But I'll relive happy memories,
strive to conquer my loneliness;
for the day will surely come when
we'll again share togetherness.

Lucille Jean Bielak

Aubade for Easter Day

The lyric voice of dawn-awakened bird
rings out to celebrate glad Easter Day.
Once, in the Resurrection garden stirred
the lyric voice of dawn-awakened bird,
as counterpoint to those words Mary heard,
bidding her put her anxious grief away.
The lyric voice of dawn-awakened bird
rings out to celebrate glad Easter Day.

Barbara Wilcock Bland

Broad is the Way

Time was when each town was a distinct entity;
when individuals were saved by grace.
Now progress gives us motorways in quantity,
connecting clones of every other place,
and clever talkers twitter that the race
of Mortal men is less important than
that ozone layer. Who can have the face
to say souls matter more than gas? I can!

Shall aerosols impair Lord God's own plan?
Or traffic aimed for towns all made the same?
Christ saved the world enfleshed as perfect Man,
not gaseous spirit, as some talkers claim.

Don't let our souls forfeit their true identity,
absorbed by Hell's homogenised nonentity.

Barbara Wilcock Bland

Decision

In the background
the brook is running,
chuckling and scurrying,
tilting the pebbles.

Digging and breaking,
whispering and waking
the secret heart.

There is laughter in the water.
Clear, cold
it winds sparkling
through the moors of fear,
refreshing my soul.
And the song beckons my spirit;
it seals its beauty into my head.
Do I follow the path of water,
or turn away instead?

Jenny Booth

Blue Flowers

Way above the treeline,
where the sun has long given up
trying to warm the thin air,
small blue flowers grow
in the shadows of cold grey rock.
All summer they have waited
for someone to find them;
all along their purpose clear –
to tell all those who have wandered
on an alternative path that
God's love is everywhere.

Idris Caffrey

Once Again

Sometimes we suddenly see things
that for too long have been away.

Through tall tangled trees
I make out the church again –
black as a crow rising to meet morning.
Maybe it was the patch of red
flaming behind its ancient presence
that drew my gaze as the cold wind came,
cut thin by the slanted towers.

Whatever it was I stumble towards
the oak doors, where I wonder
if perhaps to day God has painted
a different kind of sky because He knows
in this age we are drawn to strange things,
and with half an eye may discover
that place where we can begin to find Him.

Idris Caffrey

Choirs

The choirs start up
past midnight, smart
men in suit and tie
with bursting red faces
and mouths open like
fish synchronised in a
duplicity of sound that
fills the flapping tent
and rises like flames
to the starlit sky.
Six uncles in the front
row and two at the back –
my father's space now
empty at the side.

A rich blend of voices
that close your eyes, lets
you drift away to places
where only angels sleep.

Idris Caffrey

Finding Emily Brontë

Such a cold October day,
drystone walls, heavy with frost.
Mist swirls cloaks of mystery
around the whispers of the moors.

Beneath my boots the streets of Haworth
shiver with the ghostly steps of the past.
Gravestones hem in the ageless house,
the gate creaks as I lift the latch.

Autumn leaves brush the windows,
a clock ticks stiffly in the hall.
Spellbound, I gaze at her portrait,
hear the rustle of her skirts on the floors.

Would she have found me worthy
if I'd come, all those years ago?
Would I have had the undying faith
to have followed angel tracks in the snow?

The house now closes its doors,
seams of darkness seal every room;
but your lamp is shining strong tonight
and will burn for ever in my dreams.

Idris Caffrey

Moving Countries

So this is England
with its stone houses,
black with age,
falling to the river;
lawns green and cut
sweeping away to rose-beds
as red as blood.
This is where I have come,
to the other side of the hill,
where, even in Spring,
the sun holds its warmth
and as far as the eye can see
green fields slowly turn
a shade of yellow I have never seen.

I cross the bridge
leaving my world behind,
carrying my dreams nervously
with me to the other side.

Idris Caffrey

Love Song

Do not lead, I will not follow.
Do not blind me with your light.
Just sing to me a song of love.
Stay with me throughout the night.

Do not whisper, I won't hear you.
Do not shout, I'll turn away.
But in the silence I will listen
To your song at break of day.

Let me lean upon your shoulder.
Shelter me beneath your wings
And sing to me a song of love,
Of all the small and gentle things.

Walk beside me in my lifetime,
Through the passing of my years.
Sing to me a song of love.
Take away my doubts and fears.

Let me be your close companion
And when my life is at its end,
I'll sing to you a song of love,
My God, my Saviour and my Friend.

Bonnie Calway

Seasons

Summer's joyful sounds and sights.
Lengthening days and perfumed nights.
Children's laughter fills the air
    and You are there.

Autumn leaves surrendered lie.
Fiery suns in splendour die.
A sadness in the misty air
    and You are there.

Flakes of snow from winter skies.
Webs of lace to blind the eyes.
Stillness in the frosty air
    and You are there.

Golden trumpets herald spring.
Joyous birds in triumph sing.
Resurrection in the air
    and You are there.

Lord of Seasons, Life to me.
By Your blood You set me free
to see Your glory everywhere,
    to know You're there.

Bonnie Calway

The Perfect Man

I was looking for the perfect man,
    and sure that there must be,
a man whom I could love and trust,
    a man who'd care for me.

I was looking for the perfect man,
    who'd know my hopes and fears,
a man to share my happy tomes,
    or brush away my tears.

I was looking for the perfect man.
    Was it too much to expect?
A good and kind and gentle man,
    a man I could respect.

I was looking for the perfect man,
    who'd never cheat or lie;
who'd walk beside me all my life
    until the day I die.

And then one day I found Him.
    I knew He was the one.
His name is Jesus Christ, my Lord,
    God's beloved Son.

Bonnie Calway

Behind the Silver Lining

I offer the world
a bright smile,
but not far behind
is a veil of tears
falling, unseen.

I offer these to you, Lord,
not to wipe away
but to share with me.
Weep with me,
breathe each painful breath with me.

Then through the mist, I glimpse
darkness silver-lined.
You bid me look behind the cloud –
there's more than the shining edges.

Break through my brittle smile
and veil of tears,
pour your beams of healing light
into my aching heart.

Let your light
transform my smile, illumine my soul,
and I'll give what I once couldn't give –
God loving me,
I'll offer the world my love.

Mary Care

My Small Corner

My church is like a home to me,
I've known it since a child;
my friends there are my family,
who share times rough and mild.

Small and plain, brick-built it stands
in a suburban street;
and those who worship on its land
are happy when they meet.

They've sung their hymns there for decades,
sometimes by voices few;
but God's Word in it never fades
for those sat in the pew.

And as they take the bread and wine
and bow their heads to pray,
old and young they all combine
to praise God on His Day.

The children have their special place,
and taught the way to live;
while older ones with slower pace
also their offerings give.

God's house has been a welcome sight
for those with doubts and fears;
they find a haven day or night
where joy replaces tears.

For in this corner with His Son,
God sits upon His throne;
His Kingdom grows and carries on
in hearts and not in stone.

Mary Care

Conundrum

Christ died for me – why?
So that my life is 'to be' and not 'to have'?
To 'save' me? To make me 'better'?
To 'change' me, perhaps?
Expressed like that – no.
To suit me (as everyone else), the inconvenient
first has to be conveniently wrapped.

Christ died for me – why?
To save me from myself?
To make me better as my true being?
To change me into my fulfilment?
Expressed like that – maybe.
But first I must reject the lie I know I live,
that I am (against the evidence) sufficient to myself.

A. B. Challen

Lullaby for a Young Child

Goodnight! And sleep well through the night.
The rosy twilight's gone,
the moon is high and round and white,
and God is looking on.

Goodnight! Now close your eyes, and sleep
in God's own tenderness;
all's tenderness, whole hours will creep,
slowed hours for God to bless.

Goodnight! And dream well till the light
of new-day lights the morning.
Goodnight! Till stars, in heaven's height,
all vanish in day's dawning.

John Chappell

Christmas Day

Now hear these sounds of Christmas Day:
the ships' bells and the rowing,
the feathering waters in the bay,
the seabirds' cries, soft snowing.

Now see these solemn faces filled
with light and wonder waking;
the village, and the distance hilled,
the sight of snowflakes flaking.

Now sing the praise of Christmas Day,
great choruses now singing;
good people stooping here to pray,
and churchbells freely ringing.

John Chappell

If Anyone Hears My Voice

If anyone hears my voice today
and opens up the door;
then I will come and eat with him
and love him evermore.

Yes, I've been waiting patiently
to speak to each hard heart;
just longing that all might know my name
and make a new fresh start.

I was knocking gently yesterday,
you were in but did not hear;
I desired to be so close to you,
but you would not let me near.

I waited, watched over you through the night,
to bring you peace and calm;
I wanted to bless and keep you safe,
protect you from all harm.

I lovingly stayed till morning's dawn,
but you didn't wake and see;
and all the day you had so much to do
you didn't acknowledge me.

But I'm still knocking that you might know
I want to be your friend;
and I shall wait for you each day
until the very end.

You've only got to hear my voice
and let me come to stay;
then I would show you my father's love,
and live in you every day.

John Christopher

Zacchaeus the Tax Collector

Zacchaeus collected taxes each day
and was a wealthy young man;
when he found that our Lord was passing his way
he said: 'I'll be there if I can.'

But Zacchaeus was so stocky and small,
and the crowds quite blocked out his view;
yet, determined to see our dear Lord above all,
he considered what next he must do.

'If I climb on high, I can watch him from there,'
he thought as he shinned up a tree;
and Jesus looked up as he walked underneath
and said: 'Come down here to me.'

He said he'd walk round to Zacchaeus's home
and dine with him that very day;
'He goes as the guest of a sinner, tut, tut!'
he heard all the Pharisees say.

Zacchaeus confessed and told Jesus the truth,
'I'll give half my goods to the poor,
and then those I've cheated, I swear I'll pay back
each one at least four times more!'

Then gently, our Lord said: 'Zacchaeus, my son,
when we give and don't count the cost,
salvation has come; for the Son of Man came
down to earth to seek those who are lost.'

John Christopher

How Rich a Harvest

How rich a harvest has God given,
oats and barley, wheat;
He sees our every need and knows
the world must always eat.

He sends the sun and showers of rain,
to make our green crops grow;
but man himself must play his part,
his harvest he must sow.

And man must also live at peace
and put aside all greed;
this world was made for all to share
and none should be in need.

Yet sadly man has turned away
from our Lord God above;
the world will not be right again
until he learns to love.

Mankind must work together now,
and all in love must toil
in sowing seed and pulling plough,
then God will bless the soil.

Restore again this world, dear Lord,
and take away all sin;
guard us, guide us, keep us till
the Glorious Harvest's in.

John Christopher

God's Gift

From time to time throughout my days,
I've tried to write a verse or two
that all would read and some would praise,
but this I found was hard to do.
It seemed as though a few were blessed
by God, but I had been left out.
When writing talents He addressed,
perhaps with me He'd had a doubt.

So I set out to prove that I
could learn to write like those I've read;
and in the process I've learned why
the others were ahead instead.
I hadn't been an oversight.
A talent's something you must earn.
He hadn't taught me how to write,
because He'd taught me how to learn.

Jason Connelly

Song for Johnny Appleseed

'The spirits of our fathers will walk with your children' –
attributed to Chief Sitting Bull of the Dakota Sioux.

A wandering man,
I hold life beneath my belt
not as bowman.

Twelve swift shafts of death,
they say,
hang from his waist,
but a purse like mine
with all my worldly wealth,
a handful of polished specks,
secret of twelve slow shafts of life.
Wisdom is mine
coming in the taste of fruit
holding the specks of the sun
light travelling years
across the wastes of west
of Missouri. Andromeda
babe-in-arms nebulae
are not more bright than these
twelve shining specks all brown
and secret of living things
I leave, each place I seek my footfall rest.

Whetted knife wind of wisdom and a great cascade
of wings, rising from the ancient soil,
spirits of the fathers of this land
seeking new homes in the minds
of men swelling across the sea
to dwell on alien things.
Someday they will lie beneath
familiar skies of rosy stars hid
in the green and shifting clouds
hanging on brown sky boughs
and eat the fallen sunlight as they lie
listening to the dim ancestral wings
of spirits fastened to the ground
by friendly gods of apple trees.

Rounded spurs of sand,
where the coach ponies tumble
earth tracks to dust in grooves
of running slush when the rains
rain from alien skies, forever washing
life soil from the scoured sand spurs.
Wisdom of the rising wind of wings of geese in flight
that eyes, narrowed by the sun,
seek in the dawn after the long night watch of life;
seeking the place where the wall of timeless rock
shields from the frost north wind,
finds the place where the morning dew gives life,
holding the moon coolth of the night,
sees safe the twelve precious seeds of life.

A wandering man whose eyes
seeks the far distance,
beloved of the trees;
children tripping his feet in the clapboard towns,
dogs snapping at his heels,
I see the pattern of life with eyes
blind to dust of gold and paper bill.
That which is non-life is barren,
that which is dead is piteous,
that which is living is the only beautiful
AMEN.

Anthony Cooney

Dark Eyes

On the day he was born,
the Lord must have smiled
and showed all his love
through the eyes of a child.

So heavy his burden,
his Father's still voice,
a Path walked together,
seems the best choice.

Receive such a stranger,
for he is your brother;
show him your heart
and he'll show you another.

Please climb every mount
in the garden of dreams;
seek out your reflection
in the flow of its streams.

A leaf from the tree
in the light of the sun
will brighten the world
with the color of one.

The truth in the mirror,
don't believe any lies;
you are his child,
the one with dark eyes.

Kevin T. Coughlin

37

Snowflakes

Crystals formed from water
appear without a sound;
arriving from the heavens,
a blanket-covered ground.

Snowflakes are like people,
sculpture made with love;
the artist ever-present
watches from above.

Together they find greatness,
bright sunshine every day;
friendship lasts for ever,
snowmen melt away.

Voices sing of freedom,
each soul must be won;
spreading peace and joy
to every mother's son.

Reaching for the stars,
no mountain is too high;
the only sin of climbing
is not to ever try.

Walking on the journey,
the season growing old;
the second set of footprints
protect me from the cold.

Kevin T. Coughlin

Our Vision

Love the unwanted,
help them to see
that feeding the hungry
they turn into 'we'.

Fear turns to faith
when we nurture the lost;
and serve all our fellows
no matter the cost.

Awaken the spirit,
sing freedom and joy,
that even the dying
may dream like a boy.

Proclaim the great message –
life is worth living;
change hearts that take all
and turn them to giving.

We, as Christ's followers,
each hold a key
to unlock captive spirits,
and set them all free.

Dreamers we are,
with visions of hope,
to help those imprisoned
sever the rope.

Our Mountain is Zion,
our Temple is Love,
our Journey to Jesus,
who reigns up above.

Kevin T. Coughlin

Never Forgotten

Remember how you felt forgotten,
when nobody seemed to hear;
you prayed just asking for a friend,
but God is always near.

With Him you will never be lonely,
because He is right at your side;
in that smallest space just near you,
He is there so closely tied.

Those prayers from you will be answered
the day He hears you call;
take all the time you wish for,
For God will comfort all.

Charles G. Crew

A Mid-Line Crisis

'Forgive us our trespasses,' we pray.
This benefice so freely given
means that we can start each day
released from all those burdens built
on senseless anger, jealousy and guilt.

'As we forgive …' now these are words
rolled smoothly off the tongue.
Do we forgive so readily
the people who have done us wrong?
Or do we just compound the sin
by sticking in another pin?

I always stumble when I reach the line
that makes me feel more human than divine!

Josie Davies

The Lesson

'What are you weeping for?' he asked.
'For all things past,' I said.
'For the days of clear-eyed innocence
and the hopes that are long since dead.

For the dreams that were never realised
and a love barely touched by pain,
that would last like the sun for ever,
and would not be washed off in the rain.

For all who were there and are not ...'
'But what of those who are?
Who need to believe in a steadfast love,
and who pin their hopes on a star?'

And I saw in his eyes the wasted years
and the unmade road ahead;
and I promised there would be no more tears.
'You will learn with time,' he said.

Josie Davies

Nicodemus

Why did you come to him by night?
Around the time of shadows deep
and the soft approach of sleep.

A Pharisee can't throw his name away!
Not openly. Not by the light of day!
So, stealthily you came.

*

What did he think of you, the Prince of Light?
 Did he condone your inner fears?
 Or did your cowardice bring tears
to that wide heart that knew men's needs,
that sifted motives and unravelled deeds,

 and looked into souls.

*

Upbraidings and reproofs, they never came,
    and there you talked about re-birth
with the light of all the earth;
and cloaked your fear with darkness and with shade,
a crippling thing it is to be afraid!

so, stealthily you came.

*

How like us all you are,
how slight the bar
'twixt you and all mankind.

Shirley Dyer

Mute

Can't pray?
Won't the words come?
Dried up? Sorrowfully dumb?

Fear not,
there were others so
that stood amid the straw
the night I was born.

The ox, the ass – *they* knew,
and silently
they gave their homage due
with loving silent hearts.

And you, who hang your head,
fear not to be my Ox, my Ass,
and, in your tacit way,
pour out your love in silent song,
for soundless words are often sweet and strong.

Shirley Dyer

At the Sixth Hour

The Temple veil is rent.
Rocks are riven in the sun
and saints, long dead, their living likeness show.

Those Eyes that blessed are closed,
marble now the Hands that stretched and loved,
mute the Tongue that taught
and brought new hope.

Dark the sun,
terror in men's hearts,
and women's throats a-choke with rage and grief.

Friend watches,
mother weeps,
foreheads meet,
tear mingles salt with tear
and arms encircle as he draws her near.

The crowds shiver now
and mouths grow dry with dread.

Uneasy triumph for the Pharisee
whose stomach churns and ties itself in knots.
Triumph's flavour doesn't savour well,
and yet the reason is obscure.
But victory is flat,
the taste is dull.

Today the grey ash, the dull ember.
Tomorrow ... the blaze that won't die!

Shirley Dyer

The Cleaning Lady

He asked me to sit down
and sat quietly opposite.
We had plenty of time
and I looked behind him to
four pins and a matchbox on the dusty shelf,
one dead fag-end in the fading sun
and a single rose in a broken jar.

There were always two sides
and I had to see it differently.
We had some time,
as I stood and touched
four pins and a matchbox on the dusty shelf,
one dead fag-end in the fading sun
and a single rose in a broken jar.

It was a question of re-building
and it wouldn't be easy.
We had a little time
as I made of pattern of
four pins and a matchbox on the dusty shelf,
one dead fag-end in the fading sun
and a single rose in a broken jar.

What about next week?
But now he had to go.
There would be more time,
as I put down
four pins and a matchbox on the dusty shelf,
one dead fag-end in the fading sun
and a single rose in a broken jar.

Could she come in?
It was time to do the rooms;
and in one move
swept up
the pins and the matchbox from the dusty shelf,
the fag-end and the rose and the broken jar,
and the hurt and the pain and the next appointment.

Charles Evans

The Religious Life

Oh there was a time,
a time all right,
when the Lord spoke daily and gave me light.
I went to Mass, confessed my sins
and filled my days with saintly things;
loved my friends, hated strife
and thought I lived
the religious life.

Oh there was a time,
a time all right,
when the cups that I won were shiny bright.
I captained this and I captained that,
played on the wing and got my cap,
and the old school song, with drum and fife,
confirmed me in
the religious life.

Oh there was a time,
a time all right,
when duty called and I had to fight.
I marched the square and did the drill,
passed the course and learned to kill,
and I saw my role with gun and knife
as defender of
the religious life.

Oh there was a time,
a time all right,
when the family group was a precious sight.
I sat in the centre, and on each side
the boys who filled me with loving pride;
my daughter, too, and a lovely wife,
examples of
the religious life.

Oh there was a time,
a time all right,
when it felt I set the world alight.
I directed this and I governed that,
a chauffeured car and a bowler hat,
though they charged us with corruption rife,
I always led
the religious life.

Now is the time,
the time all right,
when the Devil lives in me as black as night.
The cups are tarnished, the photos curled,
the war is over, the flag is furled;
the children are gone and the visits rare,
and the five grandchildren are never there;
the car has gone and I left the bank
with a speech and a watch and a vote of thanks;
friends are distant, the house is sold,
sixty's passed and I'm feeling old;
had an affair and lost my wife –
and at last I live
the religious life.

Charles Evans

God Is

There is God –
you do not have to be Godless.
There is cleansing –
you do not have to be foul.
There is the Father's love –
you do not have to be loveless.
There is heaven –
a place with the Lord!

Shirley Florance

Ritual

As the knowledge of man grows broader,
so do his many creeds;
his idols are shaped in his image,
and mirror his many needs.

He clothes them with noise and with beauty,
with ritual, music and fire;
seeing not as he kneels at their altars
that he worships his own desire.

Shirley Florance

Strange Altars

We worship at strange altars, God,
in modern pagan life;
our new gods bring us breakdown,
chaos, social strife.

We worship at strange altars, God,
our materialistic age;
new homes, new cars, new everything,
the latest is the rage.

We worship at strange altars, God,
abuse our sex desires,
fail to use aright your gift,
consumed by inner fires.

We worship at strange altars, God,
and discontentment reigns;
we want to have it all our way,
bemused by all our gains.

We worship at strange altars, God,
we worship wealth, success;
honour those who profit most,
despise the poor with less.

We worship at false altars, God,
not yours as once we did;
we worship sex and Mammon now
and other gods instead.

Shirley Florance

Beating the Doors of Heaven

Prayer beats against the doors of heaven.
I have no language but my cry.
I am in a dry, parched land,
panting for the streams of grace.
I have moments of deep unrest,
when I would serve you with a cheerful countenance,
but I cannot do it.
I fight and struggle against my sadness, but am too weak for
the conflict.

Refresh and comfort me, Lord, in my sorrow,
amid all my fears and grief.
I know that I am yours in life and in death,
that nothing can part me from you.
Therefore, O Lord, I will trust in your grace.
You will not send me away unheard.
Prayer beats against the doors of heaven.

Shirley Florance

Impatience

From the edge of my sanity
I can see my wits' end;
hopelessness arrives
like the death of a friend,
a friend who has died for me, because of me;
whose blood was pure
as his innocence.
But the world left
when they took him away
and judged him guilty;
even though they knew his heart,
revealing himself through his powers,
curing them of their blindness,
but they still could not see.
He fed them,
but they hungered still for more.
They hung him on their cross
for loving those who hated him.
Those ignorant people, those barbaric souls
killed my Savior –
and I was among them.

Mark Giarrusso

Faith

To have faith is to have hope
of coming home to a wondrous place,
with souls of those, whose earthly face
smiled with the pleasure of being
loved with grace.

How sad it is to have no faith,
no hope of greater things;
it is as if a super voice
never ever sings.

If in this life we fail to please,
or cannot live with ourselves with ease,
what more could a soul destroy
or Devil's will employ?

In us there is a special place
for us to fit a soul;
we then can shine with that touch of grace
and feel ourselves as whole.

When faith walks with us throughout our days,
unafraid we will stride life's diverse ways.

D. A. Goodchild

God Is

God *is* the Creator,
the Being,
the Unknown,
incomprehensible
to our mind.

The love,
the wonder,
the mystery
of God is
quite simply
everything.
Nothing *is* without Him.

D. A. Goodchild

Bethlehem Born

Bethlehem born,
earth of that earth
when Scripture
and Censor said so,
God's Word,
surviving Herod's hate
through a diverting dream,
grew to manhood,
and in growing
kept his dying
for a cross,
and left Christmas scarred.

David Grieve

The Holy Week Antiphons

*To be said or sung before and after
the Magnificat at Evening Prayer.
For Robin Johnson*

Palm Sunday
O King Foretold and riding on a humble donkey:
remember those who wield the rod of power,
and those who cry for justice.

Monday
O Sacrificial Lamb, who strides in passionate silence to your
execution:
remember those who suffer persecution and imprisonment.

Tuesday
O Friend of Sinners, whose glory shines in darkness:
remember those who languish in their guilt.

Wednesday
O Man of Sorrows, who weeps in tears the blood that cures
all ills:
remember those who weep alone and those who cannot weep.

Maundy Thursday
O Sustenance of Nations, who gives your body and your
blood for food:
remember those who starve and those who strive to feed them.

Good Friday
O Wounded Healer, pierced and broken on the Cross:
remember those who suffer anguish and disfigurement.

Holy Saturday
O Sharer of our Common Tomb, who slept in death:
remember us when we come with suppliant hands
to the gateway of your Kingdom.

Andrew Hawthorne

Jesus Writes in the Sand

Scratching in the sand
your own obituary. Read
what you will.

A woman forgiven.
A half-obliterated message
under the accusers' feet.

Andrew Hawthorne

The Soldier with the Spear

I

He noticed how quickly
blood dried on sun-hot steel
on a silent afternoon. The water had evaporated from
                                          the spear
like the tears from the eyes of the man's mother.
But the blood had stayed

and on its patina spreading over the blade he could see
a delicate rainbow of colours which twitched
and danced as he turned it in the light.

II

Blood on the sand
had dried to a blackness
he had not seen since the dead men's eyes
that stared at him still from foreign battlefields in
                                        occasional dreams.

The water that had also dripped
had found its way between the grains; blood cloyed
too easily, blood stayed, blood stained,
would not leave,
would not stay silent.
Perhaps, he thought, this water
would find desiccated tubers or a flower seed
dried beyond bone and bring life,
if only a little, but only to rise

to be trampled tomorrow.

Andrew Hawthorne

Wings

Oh, to catch the winds of flight
and soar where eagles go;
to leave the woes of troubled souls
behind me far below.
I'd listen to the song of birds and sail in endless flight,
then chase the sun through cloudy paths
and play with stars at night.

The boundless heavens for my home,
the breeze to lift me high,
to rise above my mortal bonds
and never have to die.
Knowing I had found the way
to trails where angels trod,
and when my wings could fly no more –
I'd take the hand of God.

C. David Hay

Call of the Wild

The call of the wild is a restless voice
of wind and sky and sea;
it beckons all – both great and small
with the yearning to be free.

It drives snow geese in autumn skies
and answers the coyote's cry;
blows in the mist of mountain crests
and lifts the eagle high.

The thunder of the river's plunge,
the whisper of the desert's dune;
nature sings a thousand songs
to her jeweled and mystic tune.

The call of the wild is a will within
to venture where few have trod,
with a captive sound that makes hearts pound –
it must be the voice of God.

C. David Hay

Landscape

The summer has come
burning on these April days,
and stillness to the high woods;
when the call of curlew and grouse
are over and the lark fallen
back to the heather;
there has come the hour
of ultimate symbols when
all things are breathless for words.

Spreads over the moor
a sky of triumphant legend
and unfulfilled adventure, the image
of the brown road through the Italian hills
where Roland saw the Emperor
journeying, and the far off
determinations of the faith draw down
a homesickness of the summer stars,
a greed for eternity.

J. F. Hildage

Three Poems of Spring

I

Decrepit elms are by a night
turned towards the foam-flecked
shores of Spring;
and senile beasts are young again
to rub their flanks against the bark
and seek the shade, that moved remote
with cold on the cropped hills;
another season glanced the fields,
and light and warmth have sensed
grass out of the mud,
and the beetle from under the stone.

II

(Architecture)
The sun is called to revive
extravagance each Spring,
and feed the bloated flowers
in hungry soil with colour;
crinkle, fluted column, cupola,
bell and dome that speak
in the concrete constrictions
our escaping hope and unselect
imaginings, until we seem to hold,
amid the deeper curve
of a thronged cup, our own
desires correlative, the purposeful
and ready face of a garden god,
and an unmapped sea beyond.

III

(Escaped Deer)
Unshaken the trees,
frost has loosened the stones
and broken walls,
farmers' fields are fresh and waiting
for Spring, the stag exploring
the bracken, the hinds
drawing up plough-land into sunshine.
Perhaps because of technological
distractions we never see them
slip past the house, or, startled
by a shadow on the curtain, hear them
clattering up the asphalt,
or realise that something infiltrates
our convenient world to which
motor cars and cycles are merely details.

J. F. Hildage

Travel Light

Travel light.
Hold not to your possessions.
The Lord owns all things;
abide in His Kingdom
and all things are yours
to meet your need.
Seek first His Kingdom
and all else He will provide.

Jesse Hillman

God is Vulnerable

God is vulnerable.
He offers Himself to humanity
without defence.

When we accept Him
He is enthroned in our hearts
and rules in our lives.

When we reject Him
He is still enthroned,
but on a Cross
and He rules from the Tree.

God is still God.

Jesse Hillman

The Wind

When have you seen the wind?
You only know it's there
by seeing what it does to clouds,
and autumn leaves, and hair.

Or, can you touch the wind?
No, but it touches you,
roughly or gently, warm or cold,
welcome or hated, too.

And can you smell the wind?
You smell the scents it brings:
a flowering meadow, a wave-swept shore
brought you on its wings.

Nor can you taste the wind,
to tell its nature thus,
but it is real, and comes to each
and everyone of us.

We just hear thunder's roar,
or whistling over sand,
or moaning down the city streets,
but do not understand.

So does God's Spirit move:
unseen, He takes my hand,
and He is real – but more than this
I do not understand.

Robert Hopkins

The Magi

We left after midnight, lest Herod's men followed,
leaving the tents and the camels behind;
leaving the servants – for Herod had bought them –
leaving the townsfolk, the kind and unkind.

Quietly we left, just ourselves and two donkeys,
leaving the theories to which we'd been chained,
leaving our hopes, and our status, our riches,
now only the gifts and the vision remained.

The clouds briefly cleared as we trotted off southwards,
the star – could we trust it still? – shone on unstained,
but we knew that it did not mean what we'd expected,
and only the gifts and the vision remained.

A poor raftered place, but our donkeys were welcomed,
we stooped to follow them into the gloom.
They snuffed at a manger, then bent their wet noses
to find other hay on the floor of the room.

A man and a girl – she so tired – asked our business.
Perhaps they and our donkeys knew better and more.
We had looked far for greatness, through palaces' portals,
it seemed strange to be with the homeless and poor.

We had looked far for God – in the high holy places,
in power of the city, at shrines in the wild –
we had sought awesome splendour, but found awesome
                                              meekness
down there in the hay, in the face of a child.
Small time then for worship. A quick whispered warning
of what we felt Herod's intentions to be,
pressing the gifts, yes, and one of the donkeys,
and more gold to cover the innkeeper's fee.

Then parted for ever.
We broke camp before daybreak
and followed forgotten paths under the rains,
the gifts gone, the vision now changed beyond knowing,
and only a glimpse of a baby remains:
the bitter–sweet memories of greatness in meekness,
of Love wrapped in smallness and weakness remains.

Robert Hopkins

Memory Loss

I remember, I remember,
but people say I don't;
try as I may to get it right,
people say I won't.
It isn't true, I really try,
and rack my brains so hard
to think of what I ought to do,
and where and how and why.
It seems as though I do forget,
my memory does go blank;
it's not deliberate, even though
you must think I'm a crank!
It really isn't any fun,
when meeting an old friend,
to give a hug, and shake a hand,
and then say: 'What's your name?'
There are many, many times
when folk hang on my brain,
remember what they've clean forgot –
and let me take the blame!
If only they would understand,
the years you still recall
are more important when you're old –
and that it happens to us all.

Peter Horsford

He Cares

Does God care when hopes are dashed against the rocks
$\qquad$ of time?

Does God care when day gives way to night through pain
$\qquad$ and grief?

Does God care when age o'ertakes the spring of youth and
$\qquad$ failing powers prevail?

Does God care when loneliness is all the comfort each new
$\qquad$ day brings forth?

Does God care when I am lost and care not if I'm found?

Does God care when plans are changed through no desire
$\qquad$ of mine?

He cares – because He, too, has trod a similar way, bereft
$\qquad$ of friends;
each step leading to His own Via Dolorosa of shame.

He cares – enough upon a cross to bear the suffering of men,
and there to feel the pain we, too, may share in part.

Because He cares, we, too, may care with Him for those
we know not, but who are known to Him.

Whose burdens break the back of strong resolve,
but who by faith and love may run the race of life,
and wear the victor's crown.

Peter Horsford

Journey Inwards

Close your eyes, reach deep inside,
open your heart, free you mind.
Travel light, clear the mess,
what you may find one can but guess.
The journey starts when we face the truth,
and throw away things of no use.
Destroy your hate, erase your shame,
find hope and love, conquer your pain.
Keep well your soul, for death is life,
a challenge to all, to rise or fall.
Make sure you see how love should be,
let good prevail, rid negativity.
Find in yourself a path to follow,
and dwell in peace; for all that matters
is the friendship and love you give and gather.
Clear the stones that block your way,
lift up your head, be proud to say:
'I believe in Truth. It's the only way.'
Open your eyes for the final run
when you see God and His only Son.

J. Hughes

Journey of Life

See the sun rise, watch as it sets;
dreaming of bliss, but, bliss, oh, to dream!
Feel in your heart pain as you grow,
understand now you reap as you sow.
Take time to reflect. Has fate played a part?
How much is your life the result of your strife?
What hold do we have as we stare at the moon?
As we blink in the sunlight, or drown in the rain?
We travel the path from birth to the grave,
collecting the things we ought not to save.
Shout from the mountains, walk through the flames,
smile through your danger, face up to the pain.
Clasp tight your hope, breathe air innocent
of love, trust and friendship, of wanting to care.
Dispel all the thunder, quench now your thirst,
don't give up the search of Truth plain to hear.
Close your eyes to the darkside and let in the light,
seek the warmth of good feeling, shut out the cold.
Be sure of each step, sink foundations of steel –
your conscience will guide you to what's right or wrong.
Then you will see the beauty of the sun going down;
then you will see Who wrote life's lovely song.

J. Hughes

The Stair

Erect and light of step,
Christ walked as though
He owned the stairway
(which He did).

But following Him,
for me was painful,
(the treads in edgeless width,
a cubit and a span –
above the clouds),
with shoulders hunched
against the wall,
an effort every time.

Then at the top He stood,
for that moment
when I saw His ankles turn,
to walk with drifted frankincense,
on level tier,
above my head.

That platform over empty space,
mere sandal-depth of roof,
a fathomless abyss below,
too eloquent of death.

To stand, to straighten,
least of all to take
that step,
to follow lightsome Christ –
too feeble and afraid I was,
too paralysed and crouching.
Shame and defeat possessed my soul,
and stayed when I awoke.
No wonder then
we pray that God
would bring us not
(myself indeed)
to trial and to test
of faith so nerveless and distraught,
of courage
so unmanned.

In name then pilgrim,
as I am, but
in substance lacking still.

Arthur Hurd

Dom Augustine

Curmudgenly old man.
White hair, vestments,
black habit steeped
in prayer.
Learning, love and
compassion all
evident in deaf ears.
So many years
professed. Host
held high in
celebration,
Eucharistic, true
to the Word.

Brian Inston
Obituary, 8.ii.97

A Candle in the Wind

The candle flutters,
life extinguished.
Death is an ever
present part of life.

In a week of national
mourning have we
forgotten what she
said and did. For
just like Jesus she
knew, whatever you
do for the least of
these, you do for me.

Coaches crash, candles
fade but new
lights are going on
all over the world.

Brian Inston
Beaminster, 9.ix.97

Passion

I could not have stood silent before Pilate
in that terrifying submission.
I would have cut my wrists
and made him wash his hands in it
as blood flowed out.
I would have torn a rose
and pierced it in the crown
and thrown the garland to a harlot,
spat terror at the jeering crowd.
I would have placed the cross on Herod
and offered that obscenity to God.
My resurrection would have bridged
the difference between death and love.
His ended death.

Bruce J. James

Out of Dark Water

Out of dark water the heron flies upward;
its lanky legs high, its neck still curved.

It travels to the land of the bittern,
where the water is clear,
and fish and frogs
are found in abundance.

The slate blue-gray of wings
and white belly and crown
are like an animal lighthouse,
flowing light into the landscape.

It moves at the speed of the stillness of eye,
and the still, still motionless will
of the creature that feeds it.

Summers are bound by the tall, hunched bird.
When it flies south, the grip of winter increases;
and the lake and the river gather their night
below the soft moons of autumn.

Bruce J. James

The Trees of the Valley

The trees flood out their leaves
and flower out their blossoms;
and, when the sun is set,
recline to sieve the winds.

The trees house the crow and rook,
and shelter squirrel and badger by the root;
and form and feed with nut and pear,
and provide shade from the sun's glare.

The trees fire in gold and red, and frost
films upon their bark, and lark
and dove become as one within them
in the calm suns of summer.

What Love flung love from hill and shore
to let them belong here? The Hand
sent down to rule and serve
is here, and sets them, before stars,
in His Mantle.

Bruce J. James

Into the Shift of White

Into the shift of white
the tree is dressed, the ground
is covered by the fall
of blossom, mounting a pattern,
formed by the wind alone.

The sky is white and blue,
the cloud moves over and around
what is to view through the window.

The fall of lightning
scars the wood and kills;
the electric death is quick
and burns to the root –
the thrill of what is free to breathe
and make complete.
Rain washes clean each day and night
by courtesy of the Divine.

In time the earth renews,
builds islands, mountains
of its own enduring. Man is to be
a sharing, incomplete yet daring
to intervene.

Bruce J. James

Frost on an Autumn Leaf

It lay open and crisp,
white sand at its tips,
and across its veins
the articulation of zero
in lines that were immeasurable,
calculus of the forming morning.

The dry umber beneath,
the assiduous ochres, were blunted with hoar;
and the parchment it was
lay lost on the asphalt,
brown and hard.

The bond to the road
mixed it with shadow,
until the sun peeled the edges,
making the island it was drenched and full;
the mutiny of dew
leaving it sodden and dull.

I have noticed how stars
move their great wholeness
around and around us,
while we are spinning away,
round and magical
as a globe in space.

But stars come near us
in the glint and brightness of frost,
and leaves fall and tell us
of times and futures
in which Light shall remain.

Bruce J. James

The Holy Land

This is the thirsty land, sun-baked and cracked
with age, a wilderness of parchment hills
and dust-caked wadis, filled
with dry stones. A landscape of the moon
where eddies of parched sand, long blown
by immemorial winds, dune-dapple
the waste of sun and shadow. Out of this wrack,
bones of the tortured rocks, grotesque, still-born
from the birth-shudders of the groaning earth
writhe, petrified in arc and arabesque.

This is the flowing land, earnest of milk
and honey, where the silken tapestry
of olive grove and vineyard
spreads its fair borders wide on either hand.
Corn-ripened valleys drenched with spun gold seas,
sun-dipped and shaded as the soft breeze stipples
and ripples the tips. On terraced hill the toil
of ages burgeons in grove and orchard,
grapes in the red-rich soil, pale olives, figs
and glowing citrus fruits among the trees.

This is the holy land. On all earth's face
no place more hallowed. Here upon this ground
where desert and garden meet,
once trod the feet of one whose coming stirred
the dry bones of shrivelled man, brought grace
to the untilled vineyards of the human race.
Here in these dusty furrows was the Word
first sown, fed by the living water from above.
Flesh covered bone, man was made new by Love,
the empty cisterns filled. Drink deep, my soul.

Kathleen Jarvis

Christmas Eve in Bethlehem, 1970

Hush! Did you hear
over the din of the traffic and voices
and clamorous noises of band and loudspeaker
that welcome the seeker to Bethlehem;
did you hear over the clatter of feet
in the cobbled street, and the chatter
of children's prattle, and maybe
the crump of a bomb or a sonic boom,
or the hum of a jet on its mission of doom;
did you hear the cry of a baby?

Look! Did you see
somewhere amid the jostle and bustle
of people, and hustle of rustling masses
of lads with their lasses in uniform jeans,
with their hollow cheeks and their nape-long hair
out in Manger square, going hither
and thither, one with another,
seeking and questing and all un-knowing
the aim of their searching and goal of their going,
did you see the face of a Mother?

Here in the heart
of the clamour and madness
and all the world's sadness and pining and longing,
where thousands are thronging in search and in quest
for a hope fulfilled and a heart at rest
in a vortex of danger,
the voice of a Mother is low and sweet,
bringing cool balm to the world's wild heat
and sleep to a babe in a manger.

Kathleen Jarvis

Streams in the Desert

Streams in the desert shall there be
and flowers in the wilderness.
The singing sands shout joyfully:
'Prepare the Path of Holiness!'

Then tired hands shall strength receive,
and those discouraged edify
when in God's power they believe,
which does the wasteland beautify.

The blind will see, the deaf will hear,
the mute their silent ways forsake,
as in the desert streams appear,
and burning sand becomes a lake.

A Highway shall be crafted there,
on which the Lord's redeemed shall make
their joyful, happy march to where
their place beside their Lord they take.

Andrew Jones

Our Certainty

Nothing can cause separation
from the love of Christ our Lord;
not distress, nor tribulation,
neither danger, nor the sword.

In our Lord's name do we suffer,
bearing burdens not our own;
but, in all things shall we conquer
through the love which did atone.

For we are by faith persuaded
of the Father's certainty,
that the hand which safely guided,
still shall lead through days to be.

Death, nor life, nor evil forces,
not things present, nor to come;
nothing separation causes
from God's love found in His Son.

Andrew Jones

Relying on Stars

He was always amongst crowds.
People guarding uncollected animals
side by side uncomfortable
with academics and world leaders.

Odd idea, men visiting, no maps –
illogically relying on stars and intuition.
His father had made the drawer he lay in;
his mother made bread and bore his words.

The local broadsheet ran stories
about moneylenders and prostitutes,
feeding a large crowd with bread,
the group of twelve, all male.

Space was tight in the darkened room
where a woman elbowed amongst them.
Touching him with balm, she breathed:
'I have never known a man like this man.'

C. Anne Jones

Lord of Our Lives

Lord of our lives
   you offer us hope.

Lord of our hearts
   you offer us love.

Lord of creation
   you gave us your glory.

Lord of our world
   you gave us your son.

C. Anne Jones

Enfolding

Enfold us
embrace us
encircle us
   with your Love.

Conquer us
confirm us
consecrate us
   with your Spirit.

Recreate us
redirect us
regenerate us
   with your Presence.

C. Anne Jones

Belief

God gave Man power, free will to shape this earth
for good or ill. He does not pre-ordain
sorrow or joy, establish each man's worth
in terms of fitness, health, freedom from pain.

His Will created spheres of moon and stars,
not static but implicit with His might.
Faith is our venture, Christ our exemplar,
bright Day that overcame the dark of Night.

M. A. B. Jones

The Sea

Lord, who once walked the heaving wave,
our refuge on life's changeful sea,
who taught disciples You could save
from raging storm when suddenly
wind lashed calm water into foam,
bring us from peril safely home.

When drifting on a trackless deep
where danger hides its secret face,
guide us to safety-lanes and keep
us free from terror by Your grace.
In tempest gently speak until
we hear and heed Your; 'Peace! Be still.'

When gusts of passion, waves of sin
disturb or overwhelm our life,
silence the turbulence within,
keep safe at bay all inward strife.
From shifting mist and restless seas
bring us to port in heaven-borne peace.

M. A. B. Jones

Hymn for Mothering Sunday

Father of all, to You we pray
for blessing on our Mothers' Day –
You, who once brought to human birth
a loving Son to walk this earth.

Your children thank You for the Love
You shower upon us from above.
Help us now in our turn to care
for mothers here and everywhere.

May we be conscious of the gift
of motherlove, and may we lift
our daily voice to sing its praise
and bear in mind that gift always.

For those who nursed and cradled us,
we bring our flowers for You to bless.
To those who feed and clothe us now,
help us to keep this childhood vow.

No grief or sorrow ever bring
but make of Love an offering.
May these our gifts a token be
of love in its fidelity.

So, Father, fill the days with joy
for mothers of each girl and boy
assembled here, whose voices raise
this hymn to you in simple praise.

M. A. B. Jones

For an Industrial Service

Lord, when at work in factory,
dark coalmine or in rolling mill,
anger prevails, help us to be
true selves again – cry: 'Peace! Be still.'

When conscience fails and we evade
the safety-rules set up to guide,
be there to warn, come to our aid,
teach us to see the other side.

When negligence results in fault
and we incline to 'let it ride',
impel us, Lord, to call a halt,
examine well the other side.

When disputes rise and we are prone
to prove our case with barren pride,
find justice in ourselves alone,
help us to see the other side.

And when all earthly work is done,
this life through constant conflict tried,
welcome us to new life begun
in triumph on the Other Side.

M. A. B. Jones

Slowing Down

Life has been tough, Lord, these many long years,
and I've had enough, Lord, of toil and of tears;
necessity drives me, though way past my prime,
I'm over the hill now and it's about time
that I put my feet up as other folk do.
I'd like to relax if it's OK with you.

For I've been too busy sometimes, Lord, to pray,
just saying goodnight at the close of each day;
although I'm a Mary, I'm more like a Martha,
and if I could sit at your feet, I'd much rather,
for you could then give me a sweet benediction,
and I could be freed from laborious restriction.

I thank you for giving me strength to go on,
but labour, dear Lord, has long ceased to be fun;
and though I don't say much (as some people do)
I try hard to base my image on you.

I'll try to do better in future, dear Lord,
I'll make time to pray and for reading your word;
and when I retire to bed for the night,
I'll hopefully say something more than 'Goodnight'.

Mary G. Kane

Born Again

'What does it mean to be 'born again'?
How is man to know?'
said Nicodemus to Jesus one night,
two thousand years ago.

Said Jesus to him: 'Well, you see it's like this.'
(He shouldn't have had to explain.
To Nicodemus, a ruler of Jews.
it should have been perfectly plain.)

'It's not a matter of 'flesh and blood',
it's not by power and not by might;
and not because you've been 'very good',
it's not by getting everything right.

It's not by 'works' or well earned 'perks',
but all of 'faith' and not of 'sight';
it's by my Spirit, through my Word,
that Regeneration comes alive, is understood.

Mary G. Kane

93

Sacred Wonder

Pass under a portal
of majestic pine
and onward between painted pillars.
Our eyes are met by ochre
and ultramarine;
whilst crimson diamonds sit
upon a golden ground.
Homilies enthral
through hoar frost
to high summer,
and each saint's day passes
with ease and serenity.
The rood screen reminds us
to reflect upon Him
who died for us.
So we pray,
recite the Paternoster
and partake of the Eucharist.
Illness may befall us
and the crop may fail;
but we still bathe in the beauty
of His bounteous Creation.

Graham Knapman

Miracle

We saw
his shimmering
form afar.
We heard
a few words
of reproach
signalling
to us
that
his time
had not yet come.
The wine flowed but
demand was too great.
The young man
seized the day
without recourse
to empty show.
He ordered
waterpots
to be filled
from yonder well;
and we assert
that liquor
drawn from them
was of finer quality
than that
which had been drawn
from one of several casks.

Graham Knapman

Martha and Mary

Martha, Mary and Lazarus,
friends of Jesus in Bethany,
looked forward to his visits,
never dreaming of things to be.

Mary listened as Jesus spoke,
to what he had to say;
Martha called: 'I need your help
or we'll have no dinner today!'

'Martha,' said Jesus, 'stop fussing.
Why must you fret and frown?
Enjoy each other's company –
just come and sit you down.

I know there is much work to do,
but I've a troubled heart;
I need my friends right here and now,
and Mary fulfils that part.'

After a while, the Lord left his friends,
to ride to Calvary;
meeting them at the foot of the Cross,
no time now for company.

Do we like Martha fuss and fret,
too busy our friends to see?
'But if you make time to comfort and help,'
said Jesus, 'you've made time for me.'

Lilian Lamb

Waiting on God

I pray and listen for your Word,
but cannot hear you speaking, Lord;
the noise of battle deafens me,
drought and hunger threaten me;
round me selfishness and greed,
hostages and folk not freed;
people cowed, Lord, every hour,
ruled by tyrants' cruel power;
wealth keeps healthy folk alive,
the starving die and don't survive;
probes and rockets heavenwards soar,
yet millions suffer on earth's floor.
New Heaven and earth are overdue;
we pray, Lord, for your promise true,
that here, in this world, heaven begins,
though thwarted by our mortal sins.

Lilian Lamb

Silent Harvest

I wish a voice within me would cry out
        and still my doubt,
pronouncing: 'I am God, be sure of me,
        have certainty.'
and I, repenting then, with head bent low
        at last would know.
But silence audible is all I hear –
        no sound comes near,
for all save beating heart and breath
        is still as death.

97

A farmer prayed to God that all his fields
              might bear full yields,
then neither set his foot nor laid a hand
              upon his land
and drove to town to pass the long delay
              till harvest day.
But when he saw that nature's bullies, weeds,
              had choked his seeds,
he cursed God, that He gave no heed nor care
              to human prayer.

Like him my work and labour I neglect
              yet fruit expect,
and falsely I accuse, when all the blame
              should bear my name.
I have the tools in plenty in the mind,
              the truth to find,
and if they rust there, hanging on the nail
              to no avail,
then silent harvest I deserve to reap
              and ever keep.

Oliver Leech

March 9th

Dark! The woods are dark,
brown and dark,
green only with tired pine,
dusty holly, choking ivy.
'But look!' says a voice beyond
the misty afternoon.
First willow's silver softness,
then dangling, trembling gold –
catkins shine by the roadside
against the dark wood.
Brown, I said?
No, dark
purple with buds pent.
Revival signs.
Next month nothing will stop
unimaginable volumes of fresh green
bursting from their holding darkness
to crown the lively wood.

Christine Leonard

On Two Journeys

Last year the snow's remains
had painted hedgerows' shadows white;
looking all wrong, they helped me understand
how, coldly facile, I could turn from pain.
Then I saw you, unafraid,
helping others face their darkest shadows,
because you knew the Son,
his joy and suffering,
his heart and living laughter.
I remember the laughter
and the way you saw good in people grow.

All this night a Spring storm howled.
We leave at first light.
Impressionists have splattered
ice-cream shadows beneath the trees,
vanilla, strawberry cream, blackcurrant sorbet,
petals shifting like the sea,
a startling waste of beauty.
And you sick, perhaps dying,
the bright blossom of your vision
in sudden disarray,
like wind-torn trees which seem to pour
their life's blood on the floor.

My heart shrieks at the cost and cries:
'Please God, this tree may fruit!'

Christine Leonard

Prayer

Please, God, make the darkness
of my mind light.
Help my eyes to see only beauty.
Help my heart to feel love.
Let my mouth be filled with kind words.
may my hands be guided to help others.
May my arms embrace my fellowmen.
May my ears hear true and not distort
what another is saying.
May my mind be clear so that all
judgement ceases.

Let Your Light be my light
and my means of aiding others.
May the beauty of that Light
raise the consciousness of mankind,
creating peace, harmony and love,
and beyond all else … compassion. Amen.

Rosella Longinotti

101

God is there Before You

God is there before you.
See, it is in the hand of nature,
the voice of nature,
the sight of nature.
God is the Creator of all that is living.
It is much more than just Mankind,
who believes he is created in God's likeness –
a direct link to God.
That may be so,
but Man has broken that link
and has distorted that likeness,
so that it is no longer there.
But there are other reflections
of God – in nature.

To find God,
first look with eyes that see clearly
and keep an open heart.

Rosella Longinotti

Prayer

Dear God, make me strong.
Send out the light of Your Love
to keep my fears at bay.
Send Your healing rays that I may
maintain a balanced harmony within.
Let Your light guide me on this often
difficult and troubled path
that is life.
Dear God, catch me when I stumble;
hold me when I fall.
Dear God, reach out a hand and pick me up
out of the darkness that occasionally
surrounds me.
Make me strong so that my doubts
never break the link to Your Light.
Dear God, shine that Light
upon the world and me. Amen.

Rosella Longinotti

Gender

We spend so much time discussing
the gender of God – as if it matters
Whom – or What! – you pray to.
It is the quality of your prayer.
It doesn't matter which God
it is addressed to –
it is the power of your belief,
your prayer for peace or healing,
your sincerity.
Sometimes we think and talk too much,
and then we forget to pray.
Perhaps within the talk
we cease to believe …

Rosella Longinotti

Wonderment

I never ceased to be amazed
how little sprigs of withered wood
which lie so cold, inanimate
and make me think they never could begin,
just when the time is right,
to stir from their hard, earthy mound
and pierce such tender little points
of silken white through solid ground.

M. K. Malloy

Now Is the Time

Past successes can be palpably pinched
    between our fingers
       like snuff.
Future hopes are but a feeble flame
    which may go out
       in one puff.
Grasp the golden present, use it,
    hold it –
       that's enough!

Mary Frances Mooney

Baptism

Little baby on my arm,
tiny, tender and frail,
God ever keep you from all harm,
so that no Evil may assail
you. Today you become a prince
of Light. Baptismal water will rinse
out every single trace
of our First Parents' disgrace.
You'll be dressed in purest
white – sacramental grace.
Angels shall rejoice at the
sight and kiss you.

Mary Frances Mooney

A Revelation

Peace never comes by longing.
To earn the pillow of peace
one has to work hard, and with
daily exercise shake off the shackles of self.

Often this can be achieved
by locking the tongue dumb,
spilling the mind empty,
knocking the senses numb.
With these devils of pettiness
exorcised
the whole being is relaxed;
a peace-pact with the ego sealed.

In this solitude – domain of the wise –
mystery's screens swing open.
Reality is revealed.

Mary Frances Mooney

Dried Berries

Dried berries hanging past their season's long-gone time,
white gloves with fingers stroking dark-green mountain sides,
dark overcast with sun above so thorough-hid,
the moss on bricks and sidewalk cracks, the evergreens;
then clouds break open wide, reveal the light above
from sun so low, so dim in orbit to the south,
as dandelion blooming bright in year's end cold
which turns to puffs of seed that scatter life abroad
in Northwest cold December, cloudy time of year.
The storm has gone, the breezes chill us just enough
to make us know that fall is past and winter's here.

The blazing, twinkling glare of moving, colored lights
that line folks' dwellings, evergreens and shrubs we pass
at night, while bringing gifts from house to friendly house;
the air so cold, you see your breath while breathing out,
then freeze your nose and lips on walks around the town;
the gloom of year contrasting starkly with the revelry
of family, homely friends and joyful passers-by;
arms filled with presents, on their way to wrap and place
beneath a tree with tinsel strung, all decorated
for the season, hung with lights, a star atop;
the parties spilling over – offices, churches, homes;
the lights, the presents, songs on radios, and carols
sung by friends and kin and folks we hardly know –
all speak of hearts connected to Eternal Light
from God above, the Giver of our lives and joys.

But others here, the homeless, friendless, elderly,
abandoned by both friends and strangers, struggling just
to keep alive the memory of hope itself;
who live each moment for the next, so desperate
that habit's all that keeps them just enough alive
to wait for friends or hand-out packages of food;
these speak of those who pass them by, forget or in
the hardness of their hearts and callousness of thought
refuse both Light and God who sends it to their steps.
No songs or lights or gifts or breath – dried berries hang.

Philip C. Moore

Light

Soft play of dappled light upon the hills
across the north, from east to farthest west,
reveals late fall of year, as wheatland spills
its colors for the viewers, who are blessed.

Veined yellow leaves of maple and the gold-
bronze leaves of giant chestnut fall to earth
as knobby trunks anticipate the cold,
and sap to rise next spring awaits rebirth.

Grim ranks of thick, gray clouds shut out the blue
of spring and summer's cheerful, brilliant skies,
as sunless days and chill now bring us to
the crest of life: has age yet made us wise?

Bright crimsons, gold and somber steel of fall
caress us ere the winter covers all.

Philip C. Moore

On the Way

Reaching the end of a journey
must be a time for reflection.
What of your conduct in passing –
would it leave hurt or affection?

Did you use others as ladders,
or were you just, honest and fair?
Halting your own progress sometimes
to give helping hands here and there.

Try to be kind as you travel,
face each day with friendly intent;
guilt feelings bred by past actions
can blemish your future content.

Cyril Mountjoy

Journey's End Hymn

God gives to each of us a life,
and with that life He grants free will;
it is for us to choose the path
to follow as we climb the hill.

The wise will keep God's star in sight,
recalling what Job had to say:
'Let faith decide each daily act,
what God gives He can take away.'

We know not when the blade will fall
to cut the cords that bind us here;
but fall it will in God's good time,
in future decades or next year.

Then we shall stand before the Judge,
called to account as the accused,
to answer for our days on earth
when time or talents were mis-used.

Cyril Mountjoy

A Moment by the Acantilado

Muss es sein? – Es muss sein!
epigraphs to the final movement of Beethoven's last quartet

A thousand feet high and reaching massively south
from Teno light to the spruce margin of a tourist haven
ten miles away, a crinkled buttress of basalt braves
onslaught of seas that unremittingly strike and seethe.
This is the Acantilado. Wandering fingers of light
fondle its riven face as the sun works round the day,
defining its ropes of rock, its clefts and courses and cavelets,
never two hours the same, yet changeless early and late.

It is worth more than a photograph from the deck of the boat
that brings its passengers to view the dolphins or take a dip
in the bay of Masca; merits more than a word from the
                                                      trippers
at lunch by the pool, who ignore the sea's incessant beat.
This is an image of time and beyond time, a sign
capturing aeons complete in the lens of a round minute
out of the ceaseless tremor of earth's primeval skin;
a moment of the eternal in this noonday's singular scene.

Out in the sound, a fisherman in his blue-gunwaled skiff
is tending his flimsy nets, making a wayward killing
on a trading floor where current trends never hold still;
one error, and the mocking breakers clap and scoff;
wise, when the storm wind prompts, out of the pallid west,
he'll run for Teno's bleak beach, or southward a mile
to Santiago, where the indispensable Virgin sits smiling
in her hut on the harbour wall, shelter from the ocean's worst.

And if I envy him it is not in some fey, addled belief
that a life of endangered toil is the virtuous life. No.
Nor will I put his decent human pretensions lower
than anyone else's to goods and ease and consoling love.
But I still think the soul of him less able to come to harm
as long as his hunched and weathered hopes remain thus oddly
poised between the stark Atlantic and the simple mother
                                                    of God.
A freeman? Free. And sentenced. In prison, at home.

But the gull that floats alone in the lee of the huge rock,
a fragile pinnace of feathers, is more at home in her dwelling,
tenanted unconcernedly on the multiforming swell
that gathers and folds like a press, stretches and tugs like a rack.
Incertitude's her element; she keeps no account of what
the tale of moment by moment will bring. Hope and despair
are foreigners from the dry domain of human feeling. Her airy
trust in the tides of sky and sea shifts not a whit.

Doubt blurs my human eye; the agnostic I
composing this instant from the truculent wild of ocean,
scowl of the cliff, stillness of fisherman and bird; a gross
consort of accidentals, diminishing to a round O –
rondo of now in time in now, a spiralling dance.
These forms converge crazily on my whorled reason.
Do I grasp a meaning that changes with light and breeze,
or am I, changeable, grasped – helpless, dunce, dense?

Dreamer or dreamed-of – that old conundrum we set
ourselves:
if dreamed-of, must I pitch into nothing when Dreamer wakes
from his terrible reverie; or if dreaming, will a daybreak
restore me to an inconceivable self? This riddle no one solves
or returns to unravel, though the question must be mine soon.
I feel the advent of a change, second by quavering second,
as the fisherman feels the sly nudge of the wind on his neck.
Time slips; the world melts; *muss es sein?*

Suddenly the gull soars, snowy-vanned, her broad
span sketching a Christ-cross on the virginal blue;
image of the soul's flight; nothing of earth pursuing,
she turns and pauses at heaven's porch like an entering bride;
es muss sein! And I proclaim the soul's existence, proclaim
against my own belief, against the coming dark; cry
how the spirit soars up again and again, flying
in the face of chaos, reaching for glory in the long climb.

Cry against the dark. Where the dragon-tailed rollers writhe,
cry. We are not made to eat, drink and fester
in black earth; clogged in the worst, cry for the best,
then disgrace show a semblance of honour, an also-runner's
wreath.
But see – the anguished second passes, the mountains stand,
their doomsday grandeur ingrained in the still impassive
features,
And green-coiled, spuming serpents roll to the beach
and welter and hiss and die in the black volcanic sand.

Walter Nash

Easter in the Pueblo

You who have this day arose
out of the cave's stale murk – the story goes –
and, leaving tell-tale on the ground
your shroud and cerements unwound,
ascended to the white
kingdom of everlasting light,

bless my dark unbelief,
my spirit masterless, my uninstructed heart
that will not lift
out of its cleft of clay, or make a shift
to grow away from grief,
or, fearing greatly, set its fears apart;

and if I have no hope to rise
into that everlasting paradise
pledged with your ancient gift of wine and bread,
let a brief earthen jubilee be mine,
this tipsy festival that turns my head –
the clustering prattle of the flame vine,

hibiscus trumpeting, the glow
of bougainvillea like a purple snow,
bright oleander's brag; but most of all,
and truest to this time, the plangent fall
of the jacaranda, violet-blue,
heavenly blue, Sir, as your mother's shawl.

Such wantonness may bring me near to you.

Walter Nash

The Gift of a Friend

Life's uncertain fleeting song
changes every day,
Yesterday the friends we had
so easily fall away.

But special are the ones you choose,
hand-picked to play their parts.
the ones that have the mutual bond
of love within their hearts.

The ones devoted by esteem,
unselfish, always there.
The ones who understand our needs,
with whom we freely share.

The friends who see another's dreams,
applaud her visions wide;
they lend support at every turn,
God's 'Yes. Go forth!' they cried.

Few and far between are they,
those cherished precious gifts,
as God extends His Hand in love
with friends we know are His.

Mary Nelson

Christmas Then and Now

On Christmas Day, two thousand years,
God sent His Son to serve.
A sinful world of self and hate
His love did not deserve.

A Servant Man, the Word of God,
to bring the hope of love;
than man might have eternal life
and dwell with Him above.

He came that time with promises
for those whose hearts would yield;
of peace and joy, of hope and love,
His Spirit has revealed.

On Christmas Day this year behold
another promise near;
that Jesus Christ of Bethlehem
will soon again appear.

Not as a humble servant
in this long-awaited hour,
but to come in clouds of glory
to rule and reign in power.

As every knee shall bow,
and every tongue confess,
that little babe of Bethlehem,
the Son of God was blessed.

Mary Nelson

The Crucifixion

Suffering in pain,
looking outwards to laughter, bearing forgiveness,
looking at faces precious, bearing sadness,
looking at a face, trusting in friendship,
knowing his love,
'Look after my mother.'

Martin Norman

'Eyes to See'

It's resting,
snug, enclosed,
between two blades of grass,
no more than ankle high,
secure in its boundaries,
yet doomed if it moves beyond them;
pure, with sparkle,
fresh complete,
only to disappear in an underground world
if it falls!
Mirroring our lives in Christ's hands,
that solitary drop of rain.

Martin Norman

Reflections in Water

Reeds blow gently in the wind,
moving with it, and not against,
resting in the soothing sound of their slithering together,
feeling the freshness all around;
just a few moments of this stillness,
a stillness from without that reaches within.
How often do we receive this,
or perceive where it comes from?

Sound enriches, and so does light,
gifts from God to stir our souls;
what variety under water –
light grey in brightness,
dark grey in shade;
light green rushes with dark green birches,
all moving as eyes gently gaze
on an upside down beauty,
which mirrors in clarity all that we can see.
So God desires to see us in this way;
but light grey merges with dark green,
and what was clear becomes obscured.
I wonder why?

Martin Norman

Repentance

Forgive me, Lord, for I have been
defiant, selfish and unclean;
forgive me, for the past has flown,
and to its hours may none return.

What but repentance can wipe clean
sin's slate, from silly to obscene?
What but your mercy, breathed so clear,
could move your presence very near?

Mercy! whose proper name is Christ!
for me, and all dust, sacrificed;
whose blood a flowing door has brought
wide open to Creation's court.

Jesus unfailing bliss imparts
to tortured souls and frightened hearts;
succeeding all our fear and strife
with laughter and abundant life.

His ministry truth's star displays,
through timed to everlasting days;
all who his simple words believe
all treasure, joy and rest receive.

For once, for all, those limbs were nailed,
and by his stripes all eras healed;
who, though on high, with us remains,
our King as well as angels' reigns.

So then with utmost certitude,
almighty Love, I come to You;
from futile dreams, dread nights, awake,
and Easter Sunday's gift partake.

Ronald Parr

In Principio

Who draws a line first makes a dot,
and bristle, paint, precede the art;
no starfish, child, without a seed,
no seed without an earlier seed.

Who reads the puzzle of the past,
and finds the mystery revealed?
We are, before the Universe,
like ants that cross computer keys.

For Science fails, still young and blurred,
and guesses, empties and pretends;
attempts great locks with broken keys
of ancient bangs and Darwin's apes.

What are these shoes, these hands, this soul,
soft nodding flowers, or iron, or ice,
but substance that for ever was?
Immortal wax in countless moulds.

Essential folly in our age
to look at Time and measure Space,
and calculate in years and days
the earliest garden's tenancy.

A thousand ages, it is true,
are just an evening, or a frown;
and all the world a little inn,
where travellers mostly sleep and dream.

From star to mote there was no start,
for Nothing cannot be a womb;
we walk a circle not a line,
live worlds the diamond on the ring.

God is inevitable.

Ronald Parr

Nativity Scene

And now at last the everlasting Word
visits his handiwork, explores his art;
all-powerful King, yet he the part prefers
of servant mild and poor, to win the heart
of crude and banished mankind. He his round,
capacious, spinning miracle now greets,
whilst dark skies sing and shepherds stand around
with beasts. Creator and creation meet.
Augustus reigns! Already two-thirds run,
man's history is a restless little tale;
the Hand that writes it puts aside his pen
for plane and saw and, finally, sharp nails.
And, in the drama of the fallen soul,
the playwright now assumes the leading role.

Ronald Parr

Love Story

I love Jesus, and Jesus loves me.

All human love must fade, and surely die away,
to leave me sad and sick at heart, and feeling all alone –
except His Love sustain me in that empty day.

I love Jesus, and Jesus loves me.

Not in some distant day that has already passed away,
nor in a future golden age that is yet to be,
but I love Jesus and He loves me in this present day.

I love Jesus, and Jesus loves me.

He loves me with a lasting love He will not take away,
but leave for me to nurture, to cherish, and help grow
in the lives of those he sends to me to love today.

I love Jesus, and Jesus loves me.

Dan Pugh

New Life

There's a brand new life awaiting
sinners who come to the Lord;
life that's eternal and lasting,
as told us in His Word.

There's a bright new Home up in Heaven,
ready for you and me,
which we will share with our Saviour
in peace through eternity.

Dan Pugh

In Memory

Altar flowers I work in memory of you.
The colours, loud as I can make them
reach under tautly gothic arches.

Other women, too, without association,
bend quiet over fragile stems that cause
some inner grief. All life is in our gift
of hands. They crumble green oasis,
untangle stems, adjust small miracles.

No voice sings. Only silence beyond graves
to the warmth where sun just catches
on each slight petal and a cloth of gold.

Celia Purcell

Where Light Is

This is a carved up earth, a crossword puzzle
of different shapes and slabs, and of grey
against green. So many tombs lost in weeds,
I know as I stand here with my heart thumping
that your name has been added to the rest
and that in this garden for the dead,
you lie far too soon. Some chrysanthemums
fall listless in a vase at your head
and people crouch weeping, the way they do
at all funerals with their long, dark clothes
as a sign of respect. I miss you now
though you are gone nowhere, but are waiting
for me over fields with your eyes long stretched
to the wind and the rain. It falls gently now,
a low, pitted sound among epitaphs and those
of us still living. I think of some word
far too late to compose, of each pattern
on stone. Beyond our murmured prayers
is a warmth from your smile that lingers
and another world dancing where the light is.

Celia Purcell

God's Fool

Let me know, Lord, You are near,
rid my heart of angst and fear;
let my goal be Your sweet life
in the midst of all my strife.

Make my meditation sweet,
let the prayers I pray complete
Your simplicity in me,
lacking all complexity.

Help me, Lord, relate to others,
loving all as sisters, brothers;
accepting people as they are,
loving without let or bar.

Help me live the present hour,
gaining from each moment power,
power to love and help this world,
lost in sin and sorrow swirled.

Let me live the here and now
in Your peace, and show me how
 to help others see Your face,
whatever time, whatever place.

And may I see Your face in others,
all I meet my sisters, brothers;
learn that I am just Your tool –
even sometimes, Lord, Your fool!

Richard D. Reddell

London, Universe

We are taught
the sky is not a pale blue dome,
the stars aren't spots of brightness
to decorate our night;
the sun doesn't revolve around us,
(though the moon does,
the sea crashing up endless
waves of desire for her).

Not that we believe it.
By day our atmosphere
spreads its deceiving hands
over our eyes,
by night our own light
suffuses orange around us,
protecting us from each other
and unwanted questions.

But once, on holiday, I saw
what our ancestors glanced at
every night, stepping out
of their own back doors:
the black night sky
explosive with stars,
constellations,
galaxies —

the universe before
my incredulous eyes,
beautiful, infinite, alien.
How can I forget it?

Angela Rigby

Rain Shower

Sometimes you hear a distant train,
police sirens, a couldn't-care-less car,
heels hurrying, or youths laughing
from a late-night party, and later,
the lonely whirr of the milkman's float.

But this was different, a sort of sigh,
the soughing of wind in trees,
a rustle that came and went,
almost the swish of a cosmic robe
on our suburban street.

When I woke the wet ground was strewn
with petals: hawthorn, wisteria, laburnum,
horse-chestnut, and feathery tree flowers
from somewhere, had thrown themselves down
like a ceremonial carpet, like confetti.

Angela Rigby

The Priest's Thought

Saints never lived
in stained-glass windows,
nor were they always
clothed in vestments.
They worked and prayed
night and day
continually.

There are saints today
around us.
They pass us by
toiling, striving,
watching, praising,
seen, yet unperceived.
We meet and greet
and touch them daily.

Oblivious now,
hereafter we
may know those whom
we knew and know unknown.

John L. W. Robinson

April Evening

The daffodils have said farewell
with messages of far away
until another Spring shall come,
a Spring that one may
never see.

Harbingers of Beauty, Love and Peace,
of something which can
never fade.
So transient the shadows are
of all that is
and may not be ...

John L. W. Robinson

Lammasday and Peter's Chains

Helen teaches her cat, Gesima

Gesima, two Feasts today
are in the Book for us to keep;
I'll tell you all about them now,
so listen, don't go off to sleep.

The first, a local English Feast
is Lammasday or Loaf Mass Day,
at church the first wheat offering,
when farmers used to come and pray,

And offer for the Holy Bread
the first-fruits of their harvest fair,
God's gifts through sun and rain and toil,
oblation blest for all to share.

And, Ges, St Peter's Chains, it is,
his great escape, it is today;
remember how the angel came,
the chains fell off, he got away!

St Peter's Chains were kept at Rome,
a church was built and took the name;
the Tower of London's Chapel, too,
its dedication is the same.

And everyone an angel has,
a blessed being, bright and fair,
a Holy Guardian send from God
to guide us, and our way prepare.

So Lammas Day and Peter's Chains,
the first of August every year,
and, Ges, remember all the time,
God's holy angel;s with us here.

                              John L. W. Robinson

St Mary's, Compton, West Sussex

Way back, in long forgotten years,
a holy house, where now we stand,
our fathers raised, for prayer and praise,
and all who wait at God's right hand.

In adoration and in joy,
a dedication of this place,
for all to honour and hold dear
was made to Mary, full of grace.

Her story in the gospels set
is there for young and old to read;
while painters, poets, artists, all
have given more for us to heed.

Mother of Christ upon the cross,
in him the martyrs through the years,
in her, all mothers suffering
for men who die, the silent tears.

Why should this be? Why should they die?
The questions asked on every hand;
this one is given, for what and why?
Could Mary even understand?

While still to day his call rings out:
'Take up the cross and journey on;
nor think to lay it down
until your total span of days is run.'

And every cross a healing holds,
for mutual comfort in despair;
and Mary's son each cross receives
for other lives his own to share.

So all may learn as Mary found,
the truest victory in defeat;
with this enigma cruel and stark,
life's mystery we're asked to meet.

Here is a song for all to sing,
a seed to plant for those to be:
a life that quickens other lives,
The Son of God for all to see.

John L. W. Robinson

Love's Many Guises

Love comes in many guises along the path of life:
the first is the devotion of each husband and each wife,
the second is affection for a daughter or a son,
the third goes to the grandchild, whom grandma dotes upon,
the fourth is for the home and the comfort that we share,
the fifth is genuine love that's always true and fair,
the sixth is the lasting kind of two hearts side by side,
the last the gift of grace. that God alone provides.

Pat Rogers

God's Purposes

God moves in a mysterious way His purpose to achieve,
He teaches us to live with joy and also how to grieve.
He gives us love and laughter, bright sunshine and the rain,
but sometimes in this changing world we have to suffer pain.
He gives the joy of parenthood, a baby on your knee,
and nature, beauty on the earth, he gave us eyes to see.
He gave us lips to sing, and smile to people passing by,
a voice to comfort and console when someone has to cry.
If we would only use these gifts to help out folks in need,
His rod and staff will comfort us, in pastures green He'll lead
on grassy banks we'll lay our heads near the sparkling stream
and we will only have to sing, to fit into His scheme,
songs of wonder at the gifts which freely He bestows,
until in heaven we find our peace where living water flows.

Pat Rogers

The Joys and Sorrows of Life

Sunshine and sadness, laughter and tears –
a mixture of both we find through the years.
Heart-rending sorrow, abundant joy –
that dreaded moment, that favourite toy;
sunshine on flowers, trees in the rain,
love lasting for ever, a heart in pain;
violence and sickness, the world's beautiful treasures,
a night filled with crying, loves's wonderful pleasures;
the birth of a baby, a drug's evil snare,
the love in a mother's eyes, pain you can't bear;
dark threatening thunder, stars in the sky,
blanketing fog, the moon, oh, so high;
blindness and deafness, a songbird in flight,
the brilliance of morning, the blackness of night;
anger, tranquillity, happiness, fears –
this is God's message but always He cares.
From this lifetime's mixture we never can hide,
until there in heaven we stand at God's side.

Pat Rogers

Christ, The Creator Spirit

When I am sad and ride upon dejection's lonely steed,
when war-drums throb within my heart as saints for peace
would plead,
I walk the wild enchanting moors; try to erase it all,
the trees on far horizon seem aloof and strangely tall.
What peace is here! A strange sweet calm, the soul's true
resting place,
as we perceive, hidden within, the Master artist's face.
A greater love than mine takes hold of all my woes and cares,
and in the twinkling of an eye my mental burden shares.
An awesome light illuminates the evening's mystic glow,
in pinks and mauves and lines of gold, creative colours flow.
I hardly dare to breathe – as if a sigh might break a spell –
for suddenly within my mind is whispered: 'All is well.'
The truth breaks through, the slumbering mind awakes to
greet the dawn.
I feel refreshed, released, set free, by Christ re-made, re-born.
We are the instruments of God. This life is like a dream –
a testing-place to prove our worth within the Master Scheme.

Enid Rogers-Kronbergs

I Will Praise You

Father, I will praise You,
even in the anger
that makes me question You.
When You heal others
and I go on
in my pain.
My heart will throb
beneath tears and sorrow
and weakened eyes.
For I know one day
this muddy flesh
will turn pristine.
And I will look back,
see through it clearly
and understand.
Hear me, Lord,
touch this body
I serve You with.
Sprinkle me with cool water
like the dew of dawn
from the spring of Your lips.
Let Your breath
fill my lungs and soul,
refreshing me.
For the battle
it grows violent
like a storm.

Though I endure
upon my Rock
where floods cannot reach,
teach me to believe
in the morning
by seeing the stars.
Teach me to see the stars
even when they are covered
by raging clouds.
And teach me always, Father,
to serve You well
while it is yet night.

Sean Sellers

The Unpeople

I am the Unman from a forgotten tribe,
a race of Unpeople, unnoticed, unsung.
My silent name is a spoken jibe,
my dreams and efforts counted dung.
Unhoused, unhomed, we are looked over,
given cruelty without conscience pangs.
Snatched away is our four-leaf clover,
respect now lynched behind us hangs.
Mercy is not mine to have,
peacefulness may never dwell.
Mine is not the right to laugh,
there are none to wish me well.

But yet forgotten, my people last,
unnoticed we live beside you here.
Unsung we walk, our heads downcast,
distantly we draw near.
We are the True.
We are the Brave.
We are the Strong.
We are the Courageous.
For each day we rise and face this life
unweaponed, undefended, alone and weak,
to face you with your gleaming knife,
to walk around you, run, and sneak
to make our unlives last the longer.
To lift higher our low-built steeple
we grow victorious, invulnerable, stronger –
the unregarded, uninvoked, unredeemable
unconquerable
Un
People.

Sean Sellers

A Lament of Death Row

I have fought hard and long
to show the world the heart within,
this thing they see so wrong,
behind my frown, behind my grin.
I have opened up my breast
to show the tender beats,
that move and push beyond this nest
to reach for greater feats
than one such as I should pledge
to desire, to dream, to care;
and I have walked the razor edge
of love to chance, to dare.

Woe, young warrior, it matters not.
The past you lived won't be forgot.
Weep, young warrior, the eyes that see
will never accept what you can be.

I have wept alone through nights,
crying for the victim child,
screaming heavenward for his rights
with weary eyes growing wild,
wishing for strength from feeble hand,
for a single voice to once be heard,
grief constricting like a vicegrip band,
and my weakened vision growing blurred.
I have awoken then to find
untouched, unchanged, the world the same,
and those who seem of like to mind
instead somehow find me to blame.

Woe, young warrior, you'll have no chance.
You'll always be judged by just a glance.
Weep, young warrior, and do not pray.
The world will accept no other way.

I have done all I know
to touch, to speak, to heal;
to let the truth within me show;
to add to life instead of kill.
I have believed in the greatest dream,
and stretched out my hand in hope
that all around me just might seem
a better place where all might cope.
I have thought the best in reach
if I kept trying to force the door;
if all I'd learned I could teach
the difference would make up before.

Woe, young warrior, forget this fight.
You'll get no say about wrong or right.
The answer for you doth herein lie –
there will be no peace until you die.

Weep, young warrior, give it up.
You're not allowed a second cup.
You spilled the first, hang your head.
The world will hate you till you're dead.

Sean Sellers

Prison Mornings

I have awoken to emptiness.
I have forgotten the scent of rain.
I have set feet upon cold floor.
I have labored against the strain.
The morning light does not come.
The walls are ever electric grey.
The clatter of steel, of keys of brass.
The rumble grating begins the day.
My body aches, my head with pain.
My eyes with blood, encircled dark.
My worn clothes each with a stain.
My lonely skin with indelible mark.
A sight, a groan, a slow-ache stretch.
A shuffle to the hard steel door.
A plastic tray, cold food, warm milk.
A belly growl, a want for more.
Cold water from a metal sink.
Lightbulbs flicker harshly bright.
Toilet roars with flush and stink.
Warped mirror distorts the sight.

This is my daily grind.
This is the world I endure.
This is why I sleep so long.
This why I dream so pure.

Sean Sellers

Brother's Prayer

My Lord, Divine Physician, hear
this a humble brother's prayer:
may your healing hand extend
and my sister's body mend;
touched the wounded part and heal,
on it put your saving seal.
You alone have all the power,
be to her a steadfast tower
in the hours of her pain;
let her see your face again,
that most holy gentle face.
Shower on her your healing grace,
give her strength to stand and walk,
laugh again and joke and talk.
Heal her, Lord, that we may praise,
and our thanks to heaven raise. Amen.

David Shrisunder

A Prayer for Love and Joy

Lord, my mind and will are weak,
worldly joys they ever seek;
Lord, you know me through and through,
help me, Lord, to seek out you.

You are all my strength and power,
fortress in my darkest hour;
Lord, you help me when dejected,
when I'm lonely and rejected.

You alone are steadfast, true,
at my side you make me new;
and the vision of your cross
makes up every earthly loss.

Lord, your love is ever near,
constant, close, you're always here;
help me try to find that love,
sent by God from heaven above.

Jesus, when you see me down,
when life seems just one long frown;
please be merciful and kind,
love and joy, Lord, let me find. Amen.

David Shrisunder

All One

Humankind is only one
of Earth's many kin,
ignoring God-made creatures
is an evil sin;
we must start to realise
all our kinsfolks' worth,
creatures of the sea and sky,
creatures of the earth.
God entrusts us with their care,
with each other's, too,
He created all of us
when He made us new.

Betty J. Silconas

God Made Spring

God made spring
to give the weary earth happiness,
the joy of re-birth.

God made spring
that nature might rebound –
his creatures, the air, the ground.

God made spring
that man might say:
'It's good to be alive, this fine spring day!'

Betty J. Silconas

Mother's Day Poem

God made flowers and trees,
stars and planets,
hummingbirds and bees,
all things beautiful;
but my mother's smiling face
is the loveliest thing I see.
God made a world
where you must have a friend;
there is no end
to my mother's love;
grace from above
shines in here eyes;
her voice is music,
her words are wise,
so it's no surprise
I love my mother!

Betty J. Silconas

145

A Time of Rest

Winter enchants.
Forest, farmland and seas
sing slumber songs
in an icy breeze.
Nature needs a rest.
God made the world
full of zest;
but we need repose,
both nature and man;
for strength revives
from rest.

Betty J. Silconas

Mortality

a poem in the Scottish dialect of Dumfrieshire

Ae wee red rose-bud rears
frae ae cluster o' flours fast-faded;
wee draps o' dew like tears
en jewels o' licht paraded.

Hud forever en memory's garden
tae temper thea passin' o' youth;
tae oor Creator, an' Earthly Warden,
mortal fear o' thea Ultimate Truth.

William Sinclair

Analogy

Thea youth-cast pebble, by day or nicht,
gently stirs thea village pond;
extendin' ripples en circles o'licht
merge elements en spiritual bond.

An auld man, thecht-wrapt en reverie,
stairts ate thea water-hen's cry;
an' tae thea drone o' ae bumble-bee
drifts backwards en Time wi' a sigh.

William Sinclair

Praise for the Creator

Most merciful and ever-loving Father,
we bow down before You.
You have made the heavens and the universe;
Your light is brighter than any star;
Your love is wider than any galaxy,
and older than all creation.
Everything belongs to You, O God.
We thank You that we are part of that creation,
through Jesus Christ, our Lord. Amen.

Elizabeth Smith

Praise to Our Lord Jesus Christ

Lord Jesus Christ, Son of God,
I believe in you and that you live.
I will follow you daily,
knowing that you love me.
In my heart there shall be gladness continuously.
I will praise you for as long as I may live,
and honour and bless your Holy Name. Amen.

Elizabeth Smith

Millennium Hymn

Two thousand years, O Christ our King:
no other mortal frame
has touched our lives as you have done,
our Babe from Bethlehem.

Two thousand years have come and gone,
O Christ our God made man;
you walked this earth, your sole desire
that we may all be one.

Two thousand years of sacrifice;
for on that cross, it's true,
you gave your life that we may live:
we live because of you.

Two thousand years of victory;
with you, O Lord, we rise,
and go in triumph on to claim
salvation as our prize.

Two thousand years of love so strong,
though to the Father gone;
your Spirit lives, your Word survives,
your Truth still marches on.

Elizabeth Smith

The Women

Powerless to effect a rescue,
not for us
the melodramatic gestures of the men.
If we had swords, would we have acted thus?
No. Mutilation's not our kind of game.
But, unlike the men, we didn't turn and flee;
we followed at a distance, doggedly,
mocked by the soldiers, jostled by the crowd …
and we were there
to hear the shattered cry that sounded like despair.
We shared her pain
when she held his body in her arms again.
And took her home, and kissed her poor wan face,
rocked her to sleep at last in our embrace
and waited all the night
and all the Sabbath for the first sad light
of the ensuing day;
and then, with spices, we were on our way.
Burial and birth we know,
but, as we neared the place, mist cleared.
We saw the stone rolled back
and hesitated by the yawning black
mouth; then we went in,
groping to find only an empty shroud.
Suddenly, there was light. Warmth glowed.
Reborn we left the cave
and ran home, laughing aloud.

But one stayed behind,
Magdalene. Was it tears that made her blind?
She told us later that she had to stay
close to that place where her beloved lay.
So she was the first to meet him,
to undo the traitor's kiss and greet him.
We thought it right
she should be chosen for delight.
But when she told the men,
incredulous of her as us, they jeered and then
ran off to see for themselves. The rest is told.
But remember, though men recount the story,
we women were the first to see the glory.

Joan Sheridan Smith

The Harlot's Story

I was deflowered when I was only twelve.
My father sold me to a travelling merchant,
a Greek from Syracuse. We were so poor;
my mother sick, father unfit to work
since falling from a roof – and four young brothers.
I was the eldest. I can't really blame him,
though at the time, frightened and hurt,
I felt betrayed. My master, not unkind,
fed me and clothed me.... Silks such as I'd seen
on wealthy Roman girls caressed my skin.
I ate Smyrna figs, drank golden wine.

When he moved on, my master gave me
to a young friend of his. Tall, dark and lean
and beautiful. (My master, fat and old,
disgusted me.) I gave myself with joy
to my new lover. He was arrogant,
cruel, and sudden, used me like a toy
to be enjoyed or flung aside at will.
Sometimes indulgent, sometimes violent.
And yet I loved him, wept quite desolate
when I was cast aside. That day he gave me
a parting gift. He had it, so he said,
from his dead mother. An alabaster vase,
smooth, creamy-sided, with a marble stopper.
He told me it was filled with priceless nard.
'Keep it for your next lover.'… My next man
I can't remember now, so many since
and none of them was like my second one.
I didn't even know his name. His gift
I kept and cherished. No one knew of it …

And so my life passed on from man to man.
I became rich. I entertained my 'friends'
in my own house. I kept my parents
until they died, supplied my brothers
while they were children. When they grew up
they all disowned me. I was quite alone.
Women avoided me. Men, though contemptuous,
eyed me with lust. I knew my sin
kept me from God, excluded from the Temple.

One day, outside my window
I heard excited voices. I leaned out,
veiling my face. There stood a young Rabbi,
surrounded by a crowd. Kneeling before him
a woman. Hostile murmurs from the crowd.
Whoever she was, it seemed she was in trouble.
I couldn't catch her words, but I saw him
do something quite astonishing. He took
her hand and raised her up. I heard his words:
'Your faith has healed you, daughter. Go in peace.'

I never heard a man
speak in this way, or look directly,
facing the woman kindly like a friend.
His voice was warm, approving,
but not the way most men admire a woman.
He wanted nothing from her, that was plain.
He passed on ... out of sight. At once I seized
some clothes and jewels and ran after him.
I followed the crowd although I didn't dare
to come too near. Face veiled, I listened.

He spoke of God, a God who welcomed sinners,
Who loved the poor, Who offered liberty.
He told the story of a man whose son
debauched himself and wasted all he had –
and then his father ran to welcome him
when he came home a beggar. God was like
that father, this man said. His touch cured blindness,
calmed evil spirits. Sometimes he was harsh
against the Pharisees. I loved him for it,
but feared for him, they were so powerful.

More and more I turned from my past life. I longed
to change it, but needed his forgiveness,
his healing power, but never could get near.
Then I heard Simon's invitation. A noted Pharisee.
Was he out to trap the Rabbi? But he accepted.
I knew what I must do. I longed to give myself
in love to this most loving man; the sign
of my new life would be
my cherished alabaster vase. I ran home for it.

When I got past their staring eyes, I saw him,
and close at last, and overwhelmed with joy,
broke open my sealed jar; I couldn't wait
for that tight stopper. Nard came pouring out
and mingled with my tears ...

Joan Sheridan Smith

Our Home

We all know we're gonna die,
but there's a home in yonder sky.
Is no reason for despair,
know our God is waitin' there.

We consider all above,
know He is a God of love.
Has a presence everywhere
'cause He is a God of care.

If your life is out of trim,
need to stop and talk with Him.
We can have a troubled hour,
give it to a higher power.

Ant time we have despair
God will hear and answer prayer.
Need to say it every day,
it will help you on life's way.

Live a life of toil and fear,
you won't make your ninety year.
can only think it is sublime,
when we cross the River of Time.

George Statham

Care with Kindness

When you only have a little,
a lot can seem too much,
and overwhelming kindness
cause actual hurting, such
as to bring rejection.

When gardeners need a little rain,
a shower is a flood;
and, often, well meant comfort
does anything but good
or give protection.

As shouting in the silence
can deafen fragile ears;
and boisterous party playmates
reduce a child to tears,
and bring dejection.

So, caution when you're doing good;
take care to take some care,
to think before you bustle in,
are you really needed there
to gain acceptance?

Richard E. Stoyles

The Awareness

My life was full, or so I thought,
replete with happiness and love.
Nothing was missing that I knew,
nor could prepare me for the Dove.

A sudden warmth enveloped me;
whence did it come? What did it mean?
No thought of God in two score years –
is this for real, or just a dream?

Within my heart the glowing tide
of wonder and, throughout it all,
the gentle, silent voice repeating:
'Listen to the Saviour's call.'

Why me? Why now? What for?
What can this failing body do?
How can I serve or make amends,
my span of life so nearly through?

'Write me a song, a song of Praise;
tell all around these wondrous things;
take up your pen and put towards
the heartfelt song your soul will sing.'

Richard E. Stoyles

Suddenly!

GOD SPEAKS –
and suddenly light appears,
dark times just cannot persist;
my soul has been long waiting
for such a time as this.

GOD SPEAKS –
and suddenly miracles happen,
suddenly dreams come true;
the season of suddenly is finally here,
bringing joy for the pain I've been through.

GOD SPEAKS –
and suddenly the wind ceases to blow,
suddenly the storm subsides;
had I not stood firm
through the wind and the storm
my suddenly would have been denied.

Suddenly,
my mouth fills with laughter,
praising God for the things He has done,
fulfilling needs and desires I've prayed for.
I'm so glad that suddenly has come.

Monica Taylor

The Runner

The whistle has sounded, the race has begun,
taking off like a lion, he's started to run.

He jets to the finish with blueprints in hand,
he's been chosen to carry the Master's great plan.

Looking ahead, he dashes with force,
with the knowledge of God, he's charted his course.

Head fully erect, he's running on track,
even flames of fire can not hold him back.

With wisdom before him and grace at his side,
he out-runs the Enemy with every stride.

Although he grows tired a rest he won't take,
knowing the sacrifice that he must make.

Time is essential, there's no slowing down,
in the power of the Spirit he's holding his ground.

He's a man with a vision, he'll never give in,
with his eyes on the prize, he's determined to win.

Monica Taylor

Night Nurse

The day was in bud when I drove from work,
it lay ensheathed in gauzy mist, long sepal shapes formed
coverings, translucent membranes veiling the bloom to come.

I did not see the bright unfurling morning
burst wide its parachute petals
to strike full at the height of noon.

My children batter at my sleep,
tug me awake, yeast of the day's happenings,
their skin is warm, I smell the sunlight in their hair.

Now the low late summer sun skims fields
of stubble wheat as mist rises, wraithlike,
after the shimmering ecstasy of noon.

The husk of day slips dustily to yield the grain
within the glume, the smooth cool pale gleam of moon.
The edges of the day curl and yellow round the wider rim.

Jill Thomas

Rubella Child

The hours turn away that cannot seed the untouched
moondust of your mind. Around you loom
the high smooth rounded boundaries of silence.

You are strange in your stillness, without fear,
easy under the experts' keen appraisal. Sunlight
must mean as much, both come by day, both pass.

Cared for by women, you feel wonder in the bearded
texture of a man, stroking the rough chin, intense, absorbed,
as though coaxing back a distant memory.

By day you lie for hours on the floor, tapping a
secret code upon the pipes. I think of miners trapped
beneath a fall, such sound would be a sign of hope.

At night you feel your way around the walls,
finding security in corners, seeking the door
whose singing slit blows icily between your toes.

The raft of your bed reaches the light switch where,
with a click, click, click, you charge the night with power,
sending a beacon across the void of darkness.

The light-waves flash a morse, unintelligible to us,
a pulse to flood the crater of the dark,
an unknown cry reaching out across the gulf.

Jill Thomas

The Waiting Room

Put into this downstairs room,
for convenience sake,
the two old people wait.

Old man you lie and watch the hours revolve,
the deep full beat of time means nothing new.
The trail you once followed now is cold,
    the scent has drifted.

    In a separate bed
your wife lies holding the heavy languor
of the caged beast trapped inside her breast,
she feels it gnawing outwards through her skin.

    Meanwhile
    there is much hopeful talk
    during the gentle washings of you both.

The old man made his way to the kitchen
yesterday, and his wife says she feels sure
her hurt, one day, will heal.

Jill Thomas

Intensive Care Unit

Your cardiogram like a demented climber –
all scree and lunge and avalanche – beside the bed
and your eyes open, seeing me
for the first time in weeks,
the extraordinary clarity of your look and word
like sunlight on hot stone. I have seen too many people die,
cannot mistake this brief transparent waking.

The cardiogram lurched and stared between us while
                                        we spoke.

Typical of our long relationship that I cannot
grasp exactly, cannot take comfort in
that one pure moment. You had gone
beyond anger or deceit into a molten loving
which terrifies me still, much as I want it.
And myself leaning over your bed, streaked ordinary,
                                        left behind.

Patricia Tyrrell

Upside Down

This child's hooked like an inchworm, legs apart,
gazing between. In that looped world
plants probe to root in air, lawns tickle space;
the sea clings desperate, scared of hurtling like
discarded mash from plate. The shattered stars
are flung to unimagined depths; the moon,
surfacing briefly, shivers in its distant cave.
Breeze scrapes the shallows, birds make daring plunges.
The child – rare lineage of a billion comets'
discards: oxygen, carbon, metals – shifts his legs,
his brain whirls. Truly he is food for dizziness.

Patricia Tyrrell

Night Nurse

A light itches
at the end of the corridor,
flicking on, flicking off –
patient needs the nurse.
Two hours to dawn.

I march weary feet
down the hall, silence the clicking light,
refresh the pillow, check bandages,
give cold water,
smile and speak.

Returning the dim hall
another light clicks at the other end;
once again the march.
In the grey pre-dawning
I comfort and re-position Christ.

Patricia Tyrrell

Candlemas Day

Lady, the candles for your feast are burning,
the altar flickers in the hopeful light;
consider, Lady, those outside the circle
where it is night.

Lady, consider those who do not love you,
to whom the Child's own birth and death seem vain,
divine wild grief and your heart-sworded sorrow
a useless pain.

Come, Lady, light your lantern star in souls
who do not understand and cannot see;
give them faith's candle-radiance and show them
how brilliant it can be.

Patricia Tyrrell

On Easter Monday Evening

'O, Isaac, how these nights grow chill!
Go you up to Calvary Hill.
You'll find three broken crosses there.
Just chop one up and bring it here
and light a fire before the rain.
They'll never use them three again.
Although it's not the best o' taste,
I hate to see things go to waste.

What? Only two there? O, my word!
I wonder who has had the third?'

J. H. Urwin

All God's Fault

After all, He created Adam –
and Eve – in the first place,
with power to choose.

If He hadn't, then hedgehogs
would have eaten windfall apples
and the Serpent died of boredom
tempting himself.

If God, indeed, He missed
a glorious opportunity
to pull the plug in Noah's ark.
That would have stopped
the very possibility
of concentration camps.

Just think. If He hadn't
given me free will,
I couldn't have done
those things whereof
my conscience is ashamed.

But then – if no free will,
there'd be no love, no kindliness,
no power to choose the good, the right.

If no dove to lead to Ararat,
no Mercedes to be chased
by motor-bikes. No floral tributes
nor an Abbey either.

It makes one think – and at least *I can!*

J. H. Urwin

You are Invited

'God's will,' they say when things go wrong;
but *His* will is the skylark's song,
His will the rainbow after rain,
strength to bear the lonely pain.

'That's kids,' they say, of a dropped plate;
but kids hug mum at the playground gate.
Count blessings. Count them everyone,
rejoice in all the good He's done.

He truly wills all that goes well,
and everyone is saved from hell;
He offers invitations clear,
'Come unto Me, for you are dear.'

Christmas, Easter – and the rest –
are gilt-edged cards to us expressed.
We answer those that come by post,
but not the one that matters most!

More Feasts than Fasts in Gospel pages,
truth to be trusted through the ages;
the rule of Love is life's true leaven –
God invites to share His heaven.

J. H. Urwin

Being There

Thank you for just being,
     being there for me.
I ask of you, Christ, nothing
except you'll always be
somewhere in the ether
     of the Risen Lord.
And that we stay together
in life's full accord.

Vesuvia

Forgiveness

Did Christ come a-calling upon a winter's day?
Did someone beg a favour?
And what did you say?
'No' to every question?
'No' to every plea?
Did Christ come a-calling
and did you say: 'Let be'?

When he needed helpfulness,
when he needed care,
did he ask you gently?
Were you always there?
Or did you just like Peter
turn away and sin?
Before you said: 'I'm sorry'
so Christ could let you in?

Vesuvia

A Ballad of the Worcester Christ

featuring St Wulfstan, St Richard of Wyche & Woodbine Willie

When William came from Normandy
and Saxon hopes were sunk,
the Bishop then at Worcester
was a very humble monk.
He wore a robe of sanctity,
of discipline and charity,
and the cup of holy blessing
he had always deeply drunk.
And though in England day by day
events caused palpitation,
as William exercised his his gift
for tough administration,
yet here there was stability,
impressive continuity
as Wulfstan wedded old and new
in holy permutation;
So in our need for guidance, let Wulfstan lead our search
to find a new integrity today for Worcester's Church.

When Richard dreamed of Oxford
as he worked the family farm,
and drove his team of oxen
with a merry chanted psalm;
when he dreamed of serving Jesus,
and pledged a sacred vow,
tramping the fields round Droitwich
behind his father's plough;

could he have guessed he'd minister
the Bishopric of Chichester,
defying the establishment
with Christ-inspired flair?
Could he have guessed his loyalty
to Jesus' supreme royalty
would echo down the ages
through his timeless simple prayer?
So in our need for guidance, let Richard lead our search
to find a fresh devotion today for Worcester's Church.

When Geoffrey Studdert Kennedy
resigned his Worcester vicarage
to go and fight the Devil
in the trenches of the Somme;
he took with him his cigarettes,
his prayer-book and his crucifix
to save the souls of soldiers
from the shrapnel and the bomb.
His Christ was not a general
campaigning from headquarters,
but was hanging on the old barbed wire
and crucified by mortars.
He forged his own theology
from Paschaendale geology
of mud and lice and shell-holes
and the calvaries of France;
his verse defying gods of war
and all their false romance.
So in our need for guidance, let Geoffrey lead our search
to find a faith that's relevant today for Worcester's Church.

Owen Vigeon

For a Church's Ninetieth Anniversary

'I'm ninety years old,' the grandfather said,
as he rocked in his chair by the fire;
and he puffed at his pipe and shook his grey head
and spoke of his days in the choir.
'Aye! Them were the days when they knew how to sing,
there weren't room for 'em all in the stalls;
when the lads practised thrice an' their voices would ring
right up to them Heavenly Halls.'

'But it's not like that now,' he pronounced with a sigh.
'Them youngsters 'ave got no respect;
you should've seen classes in days long gone by
before they fell into neglect.
It were summat to sing for the Church in them days
when your parsons were gentlemen all;
when your teachers were strict, an' you didn't dare laze,
an' policemen were seven-foot tall!'

'I'm ninety years young,' the old lady said,
as she put down her Bible and specs;
and sipped at her sherry and sat up in bed
to speak for her own fairer sex.
'Oh, yes! They were grand, those days long ago,
but that was a different age;
life was hard for the poor and the old, don't you know,
when folk scarcely could live on their wage.

Oh, I know people don't go to Church as they should,
but you can't hold on memory's strings;
today is exciting! If only I could
live to see what tomorrow's world brings.
The kids of today are my constant delight –
so cheerful and healthy and strong;
was it really so good for us poor little mites
to be chained to our desks all day long?

There's a young lad next door who's only sixteen,
he pops in to see me each day;
he's kindness itself, treats me just like a queen,
and brings me my tea on a tray.
If only we'd get on with loving our kids,
and loving our husbands and wives,
and loving our God and His Church as He bids,
we'll have done something good with our lives.'

She sat in her bed as bright as a pin,
and her years and her aches she defied;
she waved me goodbye with a right-handed grin –
she was paralysed all down one side.
I thought of them both and their different ways,
and the stories the two of them told;
I remembered our church in a very few days
would also be ninety years old.
And I thought: 'Here's a parable set for us all
(for a wink is as good as a nod)
will we look back on days that are now past recall –
or look to the future with God?'

Owen Vigeon

The Bromsgrove Lad

O, Worcester has its Edward,
and Stratford has its Will,
and Droitwich boasts its Richard,
whose prayer we whisper still.

So here in England's heartland
where geniuses flower,
a Bromsgrove lad penned lyric songs
of strange and lovely power.

Yet he who sang the pain of love
with singularity,
is not an Edward, Will or Dick
but known as just 'A.E.'

As if to place a barrier
between his lyric scene –
of cherries, fairs and lovely lads
and football on the green –

And the academic near-recluse
who dared not act the part,
but shared his love by proxy
with every lonely heart.

Owen Vigeon

Kristiani at Viroconium

Wroxeter in Shropshire is on the site of Viroconium, an old Roman city abandoned after the collapse of the Roman Empire in the fifth century. Christians fled westwards and established colonies in Wales and Ireland.

Each summer we would go out, my son.
No, not we citizens, but the Imperial Army,
cohort upon cohort splendidly equipped
and drilled to perfection, a sight indeed to see,
like so many sights that lie in ruin now.
We would go out and fight the barbarians.
Always we won.
We brought their leaders to the forum there
to bend beneath the yoke in servitude ...
yonder, where purple weeds cover the fractured plinth,
the very plinth on which an emperor once stood.
Those of us who read the old lettering still
can tell you the wording there. It marked his rank
and reads ... but what's the use?
You would not understand.
Your eyes reflect an emptiness
that's more profound than all the old philosophy.
My comfort now is that
your ignorance will never feel the bitter
gall of folly our old knowledge brought.
'Barbarians?' you ask. 'Who are they?'
They are us, my son, ourselves.

Did we but know we put ourselves
beneath the yoke each summer
that we brought our treasure home.
We spoiled ourselves with wealth and greed.
For in the summer that the Empire fell
there came confusion, disbelief.
That one summer we did not go out
to fight, but stayed at home in ease
watching the army march away for good,
the barbarians came to us instead.
We always knew they would, those of us
who saw the signs within ourselves.
They came in wild, unbridled hordes,
screaming undisciplined cries, crudely
undrilled and ragged, yet murderously efficient.
We were no match for them,
too far gone in sweet and easy living.
We fled who could and hid.
We left the city and the villa where they stood.
We left our household gods; or rather, so it seems,
our gods deserted us.
We had to learn afresh, through pain,
through penury, through death
of all the old life meant to us.

Our new life lies within the orbit
of this ring I wear, the fish-ring
given by the Greek who traded
wine for years with us.
It will be recognised, he said, by those we seek
who hide out there far in the west.

He spoke of another Life, another Kingdom;
practised strange rites with Bread and Wine
he and his family; spoke words of prophecy and hope.
There are others of his faith high in the hills
and west across the sea, scattered.
They alone hold fast to what is good,
better than all we lost.
And that is why we come to look our last, my son,
for you to look and learn,
before we start our journey in the dawn;
begin anew our search for life –
this time in Christ.

John Waddington-Feather

Barabbas

I'll thank him for that if nothing else.
For I tell you, mate, I thought I'd had it
when I heard 'em shout my name.
'Give us Barabbas!' I heard 'em yell
outside – an' I swear I saw hell
itself gape wide. 'What's their game?'
I thought, lying there waiting an' fit
to die with fear, blood like water,
sick in the stinkin' straw,
shivering an' biting me bleedin' fingers
to the quick. 'Give us Barabbas!' still lingers,
still chills to ice my rotten craw
like death itself. I oughter
known it was me lucky day, though.

The jailer said they would release
me. He knew how many friends
I have high up, who make amends
for all the killings that I do to please.
Like nailing witnesses not long ago
to save embarrassment from Pilate. *They'd* swear
black was white if paid enough. But Annas
has his tabs on everything what happens 'ere.
Said he'd get me off this fizzer, though it near
did for me that waiting, waiting for Caiaphas
to slip the word among his plants out there.
Then when I heard 'em scream, 'Give us Barabbas!'
I thought they meant to lynch me.
Near as damn I ever came to praying then,
hearing the guard march in again
an' turn the key. 'Come out, you swine. Yer free!'
he shouted down. 'Come out, you swine, Barabbas!'
'Yer jokin', boss,' I says to him,
waiting the kick the bastard always gave.
'The devil saves his own!'
was all he growled, an' I was shown
the open door. Outside a slave
of Annas held me up, I looked so grim,
an' told me where to go till needed
next. I didn't need twice asking.
I scarpered 'ere, and 'ere I stay
inside this safe house, waiting for pay;
hit-man hired for nailing traitors basking
under Roman rule. Rats who heeded
Roman law. Curse their gentile gods
an' law! I've sworn to kill each traitor
Jew who plays the Roman fool,
collaborates as Caesar's tool.

But who's the guy that Pilate's
hung between the two poor sods
who shared my cell with me?
Some rabbi from the north, they say, afire
with truth he claims direct from God. Some mazy
preacherman from Nazareth, they say. A crazy
carpenter who thinks he is Messiah,
him they call the Saviour-to-be.
He'll know the truth all right – but not from God. No lies
hang on the cross. Stark fact alone
hangs there, hammered with nails
as all hope ends and courage fails,
when iron splinters cracking bone
bared to the heat, and maddening flies
buzz devils round your head;
sucking the blood that soaks the cross
and cakes the hands and feet.

He'll find the truth all right through sweet
release that comes with death. His loss
my gain. His death my life, dying instead
of me. Him that Caiaphas said must die
for all of us for calling himself Messiah,
and others call the miracle-man.
But one thing's sure, he's carried the can
for me. He's gone through blood an' fire
to save us *all* – for High Priests never lie!
I'll thank him for that, if nothing else.

John Waddington-Feather

Listen to the Bells

In the
distance
church bells! Could it be?
From the citadel of faith.
Who is it
who listens
to the bells?
Listen to them peal –
they're the bells of faith.
What do they say?
Shapely as they turn
summoning to church
the faithful.
Faithful followers of Christ,
hear the bells,
understand the bells,
as they peal in the spire,
as they turn in the tower,
the citadel of faith.

Faith rings true –
the bells,
they summon you to church,
all you faithful.
Faithful followers of Christ,
come to church,
come to the church.

Listen to the bells,
the bells of faith;
comely in their shape,
they summon you to peace.
Faithful followers of Christ,
come to peace,
come to peace.
Listen to the bells;
they summon you to bliss;
seal it with His kiss,
the kiss of Jesus,
the symbol of His faith,
the faith
of Jesus.

Bill West

Let's Set the Easter-Trimmings Out

Let's set the Easter-trimmings out,
purple and yellow and green,
the colors of the spring,
when crocuses beset the lawn
like a table's offering,
purple and gold and white,
the colors of an Easter's dawn,

and let's hardboil some eggs
and put the colorings out,
some red for the Greeks and their tables in the East,
and in a basket lay some green
as in a spring-bird's nest
with hope for a chocolate hatchling
out of a marshmallow-yolk,

and, after church, it's ham with yams
or lamb with peas
on a table set for all our folk,
laid out with our table's best
on a cloth of Easter-white,
and let's sing for spring's good weather
and for the flowers' coming out.

The coming-forth of leaves
out of the winter's womb
is what Easter's all about,
the coming-back of Jesus
from three days in the tomb,
the coming back of life,
the ending of all doubt,
as the wind shifts to the south.

Bill West

To the Angel of the Church at ?

To the angel of some local congregation
    Jesus, the Risen, nowadays might say:
'How is the current lampstand situation?
    And are you well adjusted
to let in my living brightness,
    and turn man's night to day?'

'Our tiny candlestick of organisation
    burns at both ends, Lord. We all feel drained and dry.
We suffer a strange syndrome, virtual immolation.
    Lord, even now we're facing
terminal energy-crisis.
    Dear Lord, we can't think why.'

'O, slow of heart, I, source of all Creation,
    energy endless, unquenched, sure supply,
unconsumed fuel of Moses' revelation,
    I am the Church's power point.
Receive my Spirit, lampstand –
    or all your light will die!'

Grace Westerduin

My Mother

As you went through that door
to widowhood's estate,
I kissed you, as if greeting a bride
through the arch of the chancel.

The lark sang glory to God.
Your loss was elevated
from the deadly crypt of grief
to heaven's clerestory – thanksgiving.

A rainbow's promise spanned that hour,
as it had their well-shared
lifetime. 'Happily ever after'
death's night could not diminish.

Composed, gently reflective,
in the sunset after his funeral,
you whispered, calm and radiant:
'What a beautiful celebration!'

Grace Westerduin

I Can Hear You Calling

I can hear you calling through the mountains,
your words come ever gently to my heart.
Your voice reaches into darkest domains,
to depths long unsounded, still far apart.

In the morning when the sun comes streaming,
you will draw me homewards to your heart,
to where the source of all is gleaming,
to the point of my life's forgotten start.

A. K. Whitehead

Inventions

They see in the burning bush a natural phenomenon,
set alight by the imagination;
walking on water as a chemical reaction;
feeding the five thousand as unpacking packed lunches
(and the four as literary repetition);
and they wonder why they have no faith,
when the precursor of faith is belief –
and both a consequence of meeting, encountering,
accepting an unimaginably greater Power.

A. K. Whitehead

Exposure

The one event that changed my life
was meeting with the Holy Spirit.
He 'stood' as though some feet away
and radiated love –
love as I have never known,
never suspected,
never thought to experience.
He *is* love, of course, but unlike ours:
no insular prevarication,
nor turning every situation into opportunity
for accumulating selfness;
nor each defenceless moment
into a capture of a piece of someone else.
He gave, not took, nor could it be otherwise,
because it is His nature. He made no demands for change,
but by His very presence changed,
as though a fire burned before a candle
weakly lit with bending wick,
melting but re-forming wax in the generated glow,
yet transforming from within.

An event so real that nothing else was ever real,
but dreamlike things before one's birth;
vaguely beheld through muffled confines of the womb,
sounds defused from sightless things
that could not touch nor be touched,
unseen and indistinctly heard, mere vagaries
and echoing fragments of an unperceived reality.

So it seemed was everything before,
while now life was fresh and real
and bursting joy transcending hope;
for everything was realised and contained
within the breadth and breath of those few moments.

Exposure to all that was forever real as nothing else;
a soul stretched out like film within a camera's back,
dark and waiting for an opening shutter
that flooded in the love like light,
and burned the images indelibly in colour and in form,
so that the film could never be the same again,
nor ever wished to be.

A. K. Whitehead

Unity

Mary, Mother of God,
Mother of mine,
how long I pined –
with little knowledge,
less understanding
of your human touch.

Mary, Mother of God,
Mother of mine,
once I followed the Jesus Way –
faltering, stumbling, falling.
The only way I knew!

Now, the extended light of Mary shines,
smoothing my path;
steadying me
along the Jesus way –
bonding father, mother, daughter, son.

In the unity of the Holy Spirit
I discover my true self –
restored; renewed
I need Jesus *and* Mary
filling me daily by God's grace.
This United Way
it is divine.

Wendy Whitehead

The Counsellor

To day I met my friend,
the Counsellor.
Repeated reluctance,
initial nervousness,
gave way to silence –
relief in me.

The tactful smile,
appropriate word,
prompted stirrings of new life –
observed, this time,
from a different,
more daring perspective.

Use the crisis positively,
creatively maybe?
Expectantly waiting
clear vistas to appear.
Fear not to die a little,
sweep away bruised fruit and fallen leaves.

Weather a future storm
confidently as the evergreen,
retain your dignity;
let go – move on
with God, *our* friend,
the Counsellor.

In fond embrace, I trusted her;
adventurously stepped through the open door
to cherish the healing just begun.

Wendy Whitehead

Forgive Me, Lord

Forgive me, Lord, for all my sins unto this day,
for many, many times that I have failed and turned away,
for foolish thoughts of selfish gain, and chances I have lost;
my heart is filled with sadness. Oh, the precious years
                                              they cost,

Again I know You hear me from this my lowly place.
Once more my tears are mingled as I seek You face to face.
Amid the world about me,
by those with whom I stand,
I know Your Presence with me
as I clasp *The Unseen Hand.*

                                              Jules Willis

Words

'But the word of the Lord endures for ever.' 1 Peter 1.24–25

Though many words will pass our lips along life's fretful way,
few will truly speak from deep within our hearts and say
how much we care and yearn to share what others haven't seen,
or really show with open mind a deeper love within.

Too soon the years of youth are spent and dreams must
                                            fade away.
Memories grow dim as timeless tides take out life's little day.
Engraved on memory's ancient stones we each have often read
are loving words we tried to find, but somehow never said.

Man cannot live on only bread nor feed on engraved stone,
yet all may share and truly know a love that's theirs alone.
Dare to trust and you will hear such words of love divine.
Ponder these and you will see – the pen alone is mine.

Jules Willis

A Chorister's Prayer

Here, in this your house of prayer,
teach us, Lord, to learn and share
the lessons we can each, in time,
gain from singing words that rhyme.

Help us hymns and songs to sing,
while in our lives remembering
the words our voice and lips impart
must first be felt within the heart.

Words that plead 'just as I am',
and first reveal a 'wondrous cross',
a shepherd who would 'bring a lamb',
'my richest gain I count but loss'.

Dear Lord, may we who call your name
reach out to those in fear and pain;
help us to give our prayers and time,
that they may know your love sublime.

For you see failures deep within,
yet love each one of us by choice;
not just those who sing the best,
or those who have the loudest voice!

Jules Willis